CASE STUDIES FOR PRACTICE 6

Social work in the wake of disaster

David Tumelty

Series Editor: Philip Seed

Jessica Kingsley Publishers
London

First published in the United Kingdom in 1990 by
Jessica Kingsley Publishers Ltd
118 Pentonville Road
London N1 9JN

© 1990 David Tumelty and Philip Seed

British Library Cataloguing in Publication Data
Tumelty, David
  Social work in the wake of disaster. - (Case studies for practice; 6).
  1. Great Britain. Disaster relief. Planning
  I. Title II. Seed, Philip III. Series
  363.3480941

  ISBN 1-85302-060-5
  ISSN 0955-7989

CONTENTS

Editor's Foreword

This book incorporates accounts relating to work with, and responses from, individual people affected by a particular disaster - the Piper Alpha disaster off-shore near Aberdeen. It incorporates a series of case studies within a single, larger case study. Yet the author unfolds the account in such a way as to draw on the experiences of those working in the wake of other major disasters, such as the sinking of the *Herald of Free Enterprise* and the Kings Cross fire.

Unfortunately, these have become recurring events in contemporary society, so that a new sector of social services and social work professional practice is springing up to respond in collaboration with the other emergency services.

This is, so far as I know, the first book to be published to address these issues. It will serve three main purposes. Firstly, it will offer immediate guidance - though not, as the author explains, a rigid rule book - to social service departments in preparing for an emergency service to cope with any major disaster in the future. Secondly, the book provides excellent teaching material for routine staff and students training. It will be especially relevant to tutors and students on CCETSW approved courses. Thirdly, it will give those working in the other emergency services - police, fire, ambulance workers as well as nurses and doctors and other health service workers - a better understanding of what social workers can (and cannot) do in the wake of a major disaster.

The final chapter draws attention to the fact that less spectacular disasters - for example road accidents and fires - occur regularly and affect those individuals as profoundly as a major public disaster does. The study of a major disaster gives insight into what social workers might be doing on a more routine and low-key basis all the time.

Each chapter concludes with points for discussion, drawing out the issues from each aspect of the study which connect with mainstream social work practice, as well as illustrating some aspects of this specialised field of work which are less familiar.

Dave Tumelty is well qualified to write about this topic, having helped to set up the team from whose work the case material is drawn. His fluent style of writing will also help the book to be recognised not only as the first book on this topic but, perhaps, a classic for some years to come.

Philip Seed

Chapter 1

Introduction

Social work in the wake of major disasters is an area of work that has developed rapidly over the last five years. Initially undertaken following the Valley Parade Football Ground fire in Bradford in May of 1985, when fifty-six people lost their lives, it has become a feature of post disaster work ever since.

Subsequently, Social Service departments have offered help to the bereaved and survivors following the sinking of the *Herald of Free Enterprise*, the Kings Cross tube station fire, the Hungerford shootings, the Clapham rail crash, the Piper Alpha oil rig disaster, the Lockerbie air tragedy, the aftermath of Hillsborough, and the *Marchioness*.

Following a major incident of this type the role and function of the rescue services, the fire service, the police and hospital staff are clear and accepted.

The place of social work at these times is less well defined, but it is becoming more accepted and patterns of work are emerging. Broadly speaking, the social work response to a disaster is a two part one.

First, in the short term, there is an immediate provision of telephone 'helplines', initial visits and dissemination of information. This develops in the longer term into a 'counselling' and group work approach. The structure of the longer term response has varied both in the way that teams have been organised and deployed, and in the length of the service offered. Notwithstanding these variations there is a general consistency in the pattern of response.

This volume explores the types of help which social workers offer to those affected by a disaster, and those groups of people to whom such a service is offered. The material and case studies used are drawn principally from the experience of the work carried out following the Piper Alpha disaster of July 6th 1988, when 167 oil men lost their lives in the world's worst off-shore oil disaster.

Following the introduction, the second chapter looks at the response Social Services have offered in the immediate aftermath of a major incident, the options available and some of the principal problems encountered.

Chapters three and four look at the problems involved in identifying a disaster population, gathering information and initiating longer term work. The question of highlighting significant times for those affected in the year following a major disaster is also addressed.

Chapter five includes case studies with the bereaved. Two women bereaved in the Piper Alpha disaster kept diaries for a period around fourteen months after their bereavement and these are reproduced in diagrammatic form. They also gave detailed interviews which are reproduced in full, along with the results of a questionnaire (chapter six) completed by forty-six of those bereaved in the Piper Alpha disaster.

Chapter seven comprises case studies of the survivors of Piper Alpha. Again one survivor kept a diary of a week in his life some fifteen months after the disaster. This is reproduced in diagrammatic form using social network analysis techniques. He also gave a detailed interview which is reproduced in full. Two questionnaires were also distributed, one to survivors of Piper Alpha and the other to wives of survivors and the results are discussed in chapter eight. A selection of their general comments is also included in this chapter.

Chapters nine, ten and eleven look at the counselling and group work roles which social workers can employ when seeking to work with the bereaved and survivors following a major disaster. These chapters look not only at the processes involved, but also at the practical problems in undertaking such work and additionally at the major problems confronting those bereaved by, and those who survive a major disaster.

One of the resources most favourably commented upon by both social workers and those with whom they are working in this field, is the Newsletter. Chapter twelve looks at its function, content and distribution in the wake of a disaster.

The final chapter looks at the possibilities for counselling after bereavement in less dramatic circumstances. These, while not attracting the nation's media, have an equally devastating and traumatic effect on the lives and families of those involved, as do the most public of disasters on their victims.

This volume is not intended to be a 'how to' manual for social workers confronted with developing and offering a service in such circumstances. Each disaster is unique and different in nature, scale and impact, and appropriate responses will vary accordingly. Over-elaborate plans or attempts rigorously to apply previous models will almost certainly hinder rather than help such a response.

However, certain features of post disaster work have enough similarities to make it useful to highlight them. In addition, the types of social work practice that have made a positive contribution to those affected by a disaster in the past are likely, with some modifications, to be useful to those preparing to work with such a population in the future.

Chapter 2

Immediate response

This chapter looks at how social services departments have responded in the immediate aftermath of a disaster, and the problems which confront them at this time. The first social work involvement is likely to be at the hospital to which injured and survivors are taken, and at which relatives will congregate. In recent disasters, following hospital involvement, the initial social service response has been to establish telephone helplines.

Helplines

These helpline numbers, publicised by letter and leaflet, but more importantly via television, radio and the Press are often the first point of contact between the affected population and the Social Services. They will be one of a series of numbers being published and problems can arise if people, desperate for information, get confusing or contradictory messages from different sources. In almost all recent cases the Social Service numbers have been issued along with the Police emergency number, the number of the principal company involved - eg Townsend Thoresen, London Underground, Pan Am, Occidental - and the local hospital telephone number.

One problem arises because the understandable anxiety of relatives results in them not only phoning each number to try to get more information, but phoning each repeatedly to obtain updated information.

After the *Herald of Free Enterprise* disaster social workers manning their helplines were reported as 'coping with hysterical relatives, desperate for information' - that went on for four weeks.[1]

The purpose and function of that service was defined as follows:

'Heraldline is manned by Dover Social Services Department from their local office to transmit information to next of kin when bodies have been released for burial and to inform them that contact is being made with their local Social Services Department. They also ask if there is any immediate action required by Social Services.'[2]

Following the Valley Parade Football Ground fire in Bradford a similar response was undertaken.

'A special telephone line, serviced by Social Workers was set up almost immediately and through this opportunity to talk, a number of people were able to find reassurance about the normality of their feelings and reactions. Others who had been bereaved were able to be quickly put in touch with a social worker, often as a request for help with financial matters. In the first few weeks the Helpline was also inundated with offers of help.'[3]

An analysis of the first four weeks of calls following the Piper Alpha disaster shows clearly the level and nature of the requests.

PIPER ALPHA HELPLINE : ABERDEEN
8th. July '88 - 7th. August '88

Nature of Call	Total	%
Calls seeking information	217	37
Calls requesting counselling/visit	182	31
Calls offering information	66	11
Calls offering help	31	5
Calls from media	9	1
Calls - miscellaneous	89	15
Total calls	594	100

The dramatic drop in the numbers of incoming calls over the following ten days reflects the Bradford experience that the critical time for the Helpline is the first four weeks.

PIPER ALPHA HELPLINE : ABERDEEN
7th. August '88 - 18th. August '88

Nature of Call	Total	%
Calls seeking information	13	29
Calls requesting counselling/visit	11	25
Calls offering information	10	22
Calls offering help	2	4
Calls from media	1	2
Calls - miscellaneous	8	18
Total calls	45	100

An additional function which the Helpline staff can undertake is to co-ordinate with other Social Services. After the Piper Alpha disaster, Grampian Social Work Department contacted all other authorities in whose area the bereaved lived and established a link person to whom information and requests for help could be forwarded.

One possible problem with this type of service is that with the battery of emergency numbers published following a disaster, the scope for confusion is increased. This issue was highlighted in the Social Service report following the *Herald of Free Enterprise* disaster.

'No ground rules had been established for sharing information between agencies. Who was doing what for whom was obscure. Quite rightly, the police were reluctant to release possibly inaccurate information with no control on how it would be used. Townsend Thoresen was guarded because of legal complexities and financial liability issues. There was significant duplication of effort resulting in loss of privacy for some people and probable neglect of others. Survivors and relatives were sometimes under siege from a battery of police, social work, clergy, Relative Support Group and media attention.'[4]

This reflects very accurately the atmosphere of chaos, unreality, confusion and frenetic activity which are the hallmarks of the immediate post disaster period. One useful, and perhaps unique, function of the Social Work Helpline is to give people time. Most emergency numbers are intended to give or receive information quickly and then clear the line for the next call. Social Workers are able to phone distressed relatives back on a non publicised number and give them the time they need. After Piper Alpha these calls could often last up to an hour. A visit was always offered but not always accepted at that time.

Initial contacts

Other than through a publicised helpline, the first organised contact that social workers would have with those affected by a disaster is through a letter of condolence or sympathy sent to those bereaved, the injured and the survivors. The timing of this is determined by the ease with which these groups can be identified.

Following the Piper Alpha disaster, this was a relatively straightforward process, as the oil company maintained a Persons on Board list which was quickly made available. Much greater difficulties can be expected when the disaster occurs in a location, or in circumstances where such information is not available.

Grampian SWD initial response after Piper Alpha

After the Helpline was established a letter of condolence, with a leaflet enclosed, was sent to 58 next of kin and 22 survivors, [in Grampian Region], advising that a social worker would be contacting them within three weeks.

A second letter was then sent by the social worker advising of the intention to visit and giving the time and date. The letter also stated that the social worker would visit unless the person phoned to say they did not wish a visit.

· 46 of the 58 next of kin agreed to the visit.

· 20 of the 22 survivors agreed to the visit.

Of those 12 next of kin who did not wish a visit, the reasons given were varied from not wishing any help from anyone, already having family support, receiving support from GP or health visitor.

The length of these initial visits varied from a few minutes up to four hours with the average being two hours. The purpose of the visit was to assess and listen to what was needed. Each person was offered further visits; on some occasions these were accepted while with others either telephone contact was accepted or it was left for the client to renew contact.

The common themes during these visits were:

Bereaved: (a) seeking information
            (b) wishing to talk about the relationship they had with the
                deceased.

Survivors: (a) Recounting the way they had survived
            (b) Talking about those who did not make it
            (c) Feelings of guilt and isolation.

During these initial visits, other family members were referred or referred themselves. Among these were children, grandparents, parents, brothers, sisters, girlfriends, aunts, uncles and friends.

The Pro-active approach

Initiating contacts in this pro-active manner is somewhat unusual for social workers more attuned to a reactive style of work.

Social workers returning from these initial visits described very graphically their levels of anxiety, partly caused by the uncertainties regarding the levels of grief and anxiety they might meet, but also partially by the insecurity of the role they were expected to fulfill. Since they initiated the contact, it was their responsibility to define the terms of the offer and face the possibility of rejection or dismissal. This was quite different from the normal procedures where the client has to articulate his or her request and present that need for the social worker to respond to as appropriate.

A social worker described one of these initial visits as being like the first visit of her first student placement. Arriving early, checking and re-checking the address with a churning fear in the stomach about what anger and misery lay behind the door.

The expectation was almost always worse than the reality. One lady admitted the social worker saying 'this is a terrible job you've got son, I don't know how you can do it.'

Even when these initial visits were one-off and offers to continue visiting declined, the clients were able to use this to re-refer themselves at a later date when required. The leaflet on 'Coping with a major personal crisis' was also used in this way with people producing it months later as a validation for requesting help.

Significantly, and this reflects the experiences in Bradford and at Dover, people said that they were happy to have a social worker visit and found them useful, but that they would never have initiated that relationship.

It appears that people's willingness to accept help as evidenced by the extremely high take-up rates of between 80-90% is made possible by social workers adopting a pro-active approach. Put more simply, it seems that in a state of shock, grief and distress people can accept help but are not strong enough to go looking for it. This in fact matches the way in which other help is offered to those bereaved. GP's will visit the house, the priest or minister will call round and family members will travel considerable distances to offer comfort and support.

People normally willing to offer advice and support when requested will, in such circumstances, actively offer it to the bereaved.

The problems and doubts around offering a pro-active approach were highlighted by social workers in Bradford following the Valley Parade Football ground fire.

'However, promoting a pro-active approach proved to be no easy task in an organisation which accepts clients mainly on a referral basis and whose resources are already overstretched. Why are disaster victims special? Why are they different to victims of road accidents? People just want to forget - are we, by our presence, bringing back painful memories?'[5]

Setting up a team

Moving from operating a helpline to establishing a longer term disaster team is the next obvious step, but a difficult one nonetheless. The nature of the team established will partly be determined by the nature of the disaster to which it is responding. Broadly speaking the two major considerations are of timing and geography.

Timing and selection

The obvious advantage of establishing a team speedily to meet an immediate need has implications for recruitment methods and normal procedures. Disasters are no respectors of bureaucratic procedures or systems. By the time job descriptions have been devised, salary and administration costs gained the appropriate approval, adverts drafted and placed, applications received and sifted, interviews held and decisions taken, the impetus and initiative gained by a speedy establishment of the helpline could be seriously jeopardised if not lost.

Abandoning the normal selection methods and procedure for the sake of a quick response has problems too. Selection will probably not be from as wide a base as may be desirable, and may depend more on availability and willingness of applicants than on suitability and experience. Taking calculated risks is a feature of many aspects of post-disaster work, not least in this time of team selection.

Team models

Many disasters affect a population who live far from the scene of the tragedy. This was true of both the Piper Alpha disaster and the Herald of Free Enterprise tragedy. Different disaster team models were employed by the respective authorities in these cases although the geographic problem was similar.

Herald of Free Enterprise

Those affected by the *Herald of Free Enterprise* disaster, both as survivors and deceased, lived in many parts of the country. The decision in Dover was to establish two teams on a 'home' and 'away' basis. The 'home' team operated from the Herald Assistance Unit in Dover and offered counselling and group work services to the bereaved, survivors and others affected. The 'away' team contacted all those who lived outside the Kent area and set out to visit them all at least once. The sheer numbers involved made their task especially difficult.

The sinking of the *Herald* left 193 dead (38 crew and 155 passengers) and 346 survivors (42 crew and 304 passengers.)

The 'away' team comprised four full-time social workers, one part-time social worker, one part-time psychologist, one part-time art therapist/counsellor and three part-time nurses experienced in counselling.

The 'home' team - the South East Kent Counselling Team - was established with the following objectives:

1. To provide a counselling service for those affected by the disaster in the South East Kent area including all Townsend Thoresen staff.

2. To provide support for statutory and voluntary agencies, who in turn can offer support to clients in the community.

3. To aim for a one year time scale for the withdrawal of the team with other agencies as well as Social Services able to cope with ongoing counselling.

With this structure and set of objectives they set out to offer an outreach service to the bereaved, the survivors and the bereaved survivors. Their levels of contact were as follows:

Bereaved		Survivors		Bereaved survivors	
Seen	*Not seen*	*Seen*	*Not seen*	*Seen*	*Not seen*
162	28	139	52	43	6

Seen by others	Declined	Not in
11	50	15

Not contactable
10

The manager of the 'away' team commented:

(They) 'went prepared to offer to put people in touch with local counselling resources, and indeed a proportion was already receiving help, but it was an offer the large majority declined. A number elected to remain in touch, and 31% were supported with further telephone contact.

Despite our initial doubts nearly all maintained that the visit was useful and that it was easier to talk to us because next to fellow victims we most closely 'understood'. We were able to relate the experiences to other victims which restored some sense of normality of feelings.

Nearly one third of survivors declined visits. This is partly due to an apparent six-month cut-off effect. After this point survivors declined visits in accelerating numbers, accelerating further for the few who remained unvisited after Christmas - ten months on.'[6]

Piper Alpha

The 167 men who died in the fire on the Piper Alpha oil rig had also lived in all parts of the UK and abroad. The same is true of the 63 survivors of that disaster. There were clusters in the North East of Scotland, Tayside, Strathclyde and North East England, but others came from as far south as Devon and as far north as Orkney. There were also men from Canada, the US, France and West Germany.

The decision taken in this case was not to offer a direct service to those affected who lived outside the Grampian area but to take a liaising role with local Social Service Departments.

The Piper Outreach Team's main remit was to work with bereaved families and survivors within the boundaries of Grampian Region.

Nonetheless, significant numbers of people in both categories, who lived outwith this area, chose to develop links with the Aberdeen based team. The reasons given for this ranged from Aberdeen being where the event happened and the centre of things, to a feeling that the Piper Outreach Team simply knew more about it and were more in touch than their local social workers.

The Piper Outreach Team was formed on the 25th July - 19 days after the disaster - and consisted of four full-time social workers seconded from their teams for the duration and seven social workers seconded on a part-time basis from their teams. The four 'core' team were based in Aberdeen while the 'cluster' team were spread throughout the large geographical area that Grampian Region comprises.

The team identified target groups of those affected as follows:

1. Bereaved next of kin (58 within Grampian)

2. Survivors (those on platform at the time - 22 within Grampian)

3. Family/dependents

4. Other Piper Alpha workers (those on opposite shift)

5. Other oil personnel

6. Rescue workers

7. Miscellaneous

The Media

One aspect of post disaster work common to all such tragedies is the attention of the media. The world's Press, TV and radio appear to descend on the location and in the first few days and weeks to be omnipresent. There have been serious problems raised concerning the quality of some reporting after disasters, but in fact it is the sheer quantity that is almost overwhelming.

The phone calls to the Piper Alpha Helpline from the media numbered only nine in the first four weeks. The reason that number was so low was simply because they were already there and did not need to phone.

The media factor is important for the social workers for a number of reasons. First, the media's use of film, pictures and headlines will inevitably be a cause of distress, anger and concern to relatives. Interviews with survivors of a disaster can also be problematic from two viewpoints. First, in the few days after surviving such an incident, survivors are often in a false state of euphoria and relief. This does not last, but interviews they give in this period often come back to haunt them.

After the Piper disaster one survivor was asked why he jumped from the blazing rig. His answer was that it was either 'jump and try or stay and fry.' This was reproduced as a banner headline and the effect it had on the wives whose husbands died is not hard to imagine.

The social work response to a disaster will in itself be a media story, and in the immediate aftermath of Piper Alpha, and in the longer term as well, the social workers have been able, in a sense, to protect relatives to a degree by being available themselves to the Press at key times.

Points for discussion

1. Consider the main problems that might confront social workers when manning a helpline telephone number after a major incident.

2. Given the scope for confusion after a disaster consider in what ways a social work helpline can be of benefit to distressed relatives rather than add to the confusion.

3. Consider what things would be helpful in preparing for an initial visit to someone whose partner has died in a major disaster.

4. What are the main strengths and weaknesses of adopting a pro-active response in these circumstances?

5. Consider the problems of setting up a team in response to such a disaster. What kind of experience would be appropriate for team members? Would the benefits of establishing a team speedily outweigh the advantages of a more considered but delayed selection?

6. Consider some problems that the intense media interest following a disaster can cause for bereaved relatives and social workers.

References

1. The Herald Assistance Unit - A Personal Overview. Janet Johnston (Dep. Team Leader - Home Team). Dover District Council. July 1988.
2. Townsend Thorensen/Kent Social Services Report - App. 3b. Dover District Council. March 1987.
3. The Bradford City Fire Disaster - Social Services Response: Information Pack. Wendy Harrison. pp 3-4. Bradford City Council. Nov. 1987.
4. *Herald of Free Enterprise* Disaster. Dover Harbour. 009. Dover District Council. March 1987.
5. The Bradford City Fire Disaster. 'Summary Statement' p.6. 10.2. *op. cit.*
6. 'Outreach to a nation'. Peter Hodgkinson - former Manager, Herald Assistance Unit. Community Care. 15.9.88.

Chapter 3

Identifying a disaster population

After the first frenetic few weeks of the immediate response and establishing a team, the longer term perspective needs to be addressed. The broad themes of the social work task are similar from one disaster to the next, but the details vary widely depending on the individual circumstances.

Working with loss, grief and bereavement, trauma of survivors and eventually helping people to move on would constitute the broad themes, but the circumstances of the loss and the nature of the particular disaster demand different responses.

Before longer term work can begin it is essential to determine the client group or population to whom the social work effort is to be directed. This is not as easy or straightforward a task as it might at first appear. Identifying and recording information about a disaster population is a task that needs to be undertaken early and then revised and updated as developments warrant. Figure 1 gives an overview of the population affected by the Piper Alpha disaster and Figure 2 shows those affected by the death of an individual victim, 'George B'.

Categorising a disaster population

Victims of a disaster have been divided into four categories.[1] Figure 1 provides a framework for discussing the overview, including an indication of how the different groups are affected.

EVENT VICTIMS
1. Physically
2. Psychologically
3. Massive repercussions to their known world.

CONTACT VICTIMS
Those who were affected either directly or indirectly by the consequences of the disaster.

PERIPHERAL VICTIMS
Family/friends/employers of those affected within the community.

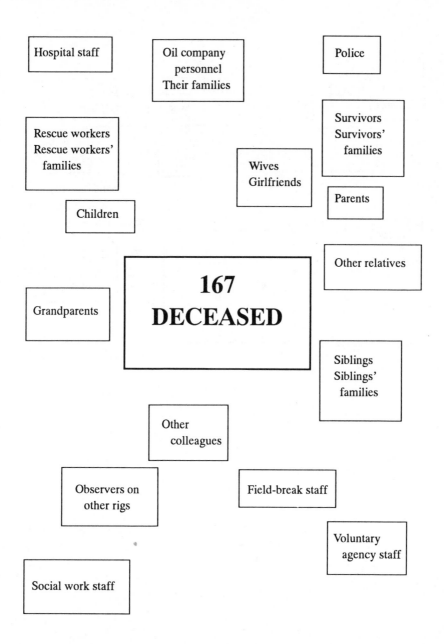

Figure 1 - Population affected by the Piper Alpha disaster: an overview

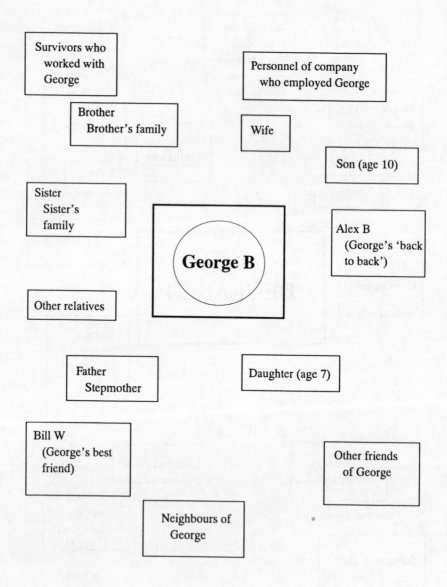

Figure 2 - People affected by the death of George B on Piper Alpha

ENTRY VICTIMS
Those who converged on the area during the crisis.

Event victims

This will primarily relate to those bereaved by a disaster and to those who survive it. Even the apparently simple (at least administratively) task of identifying the deceased and thus the bereaved next of kin, can be fraught with difficulties.

Three weeks after the *Herald of Free Enterprise* capsized there was no certainty how many bodies were still trapped inside. One year after the Kings Cross Underground fire one body still remained unidentified and unclaimed. After the Piper Alpha disaster, the fact that the Oil Company had a register of those on board did make that task simpler, although as most of the bodies were unrecovered for over four months, there were other issues complicating matters.

Next of kin

Identifying the next of kin can also be a complicated business. Following the Piper Alpha disaster, all the companies who had men on board the platform supplied the police with company records relating to those involved. As there were 29 such companies, with offices all over the UK, even this was a complex task. Some men's records listed their next of kin as their father, although they had subsequently married but not altered the records. Others had wives listed from whom they had since divorced or separated and no official record of current wife or partner existed.

There were also a number of examples of mistaken identity. This may be almost inevitable in a large scale disaster, given the confused and chaotic atmosphere of the early days. On board the Piper Alpha were a number of men who had the same surname and in a few cases some next of kin were advised that their loved one had survived when he had in fact died.

Survivors

Event victims who are survivors can be even harder to identify. Those who are physically injured and hospitalised, and those working for the involved company, if there is one, are the easiest in this respect. For that reason they are usually the first to be offered help and support.

Following the *Herald of Free Enterprise* sinking, the crew members and their families were the first to receive help from the Social Services.

A much more difficult task faced the social workers responding to the Kings Cross fire, since no-one knew just how many people had been at the underground station that evening. However, over 800 people gave evidence to the Fennel Public Inquiry into the fire.

Of the 63 men who survived the Piper Alpha disaster, 22 came from the Grampian area and received letters and offers of visits in the same way as did the next of kin. Twenty of those 22 accepted the initial offer and the other two also had contact, if less frequent, at a later date. Most said that they would probably not have referred themselves for help but were glad to be offered it and to make use of that offer.

Those bereaved who lived outside the Grampian Region and those survivors who also lived outwith the area were referred on to their local social services departments and, while most did respond, the speed of response and the level of commitment varied widely.

At least identifying the immediate survivors of Piper Alpha - those who escaped from the platform with their lives - proved relatively straightforward. They could then be approached directly by letter and leaflet in the same pro-active way as were the bereaved.

Identifying survivors of the Bradford Football ground fire, like Kings Cross, was a much less exact task. The social workers there tried to highlight their existence and service through a number of community strategies, encouraging people to come forward. In attempting to identify their population, Bradford used their local media in the first instance.

'(Other) strategies adopted have however tried to be sensitive to the fact that repeated reminders of the event can be counterproductive. So help has in some cases been offered by ensuring that other professionals in the community are kept well informed of developments...a special resource sheet has been prepared and circulated to GP's, solicitors, physiotherapists, clergy and teachers - all possible contact points for people in distress. Trust Fund officials collecting information for claims were also made aware of help available and indeed regularly referred distressed people who they met in the course of their duties.'[2]

Contact victims

Contact victims include those involved in the rescue and recovery services and those whose lives were directly affected by the disaster.

When the Piper Alpha platform exploded there were many stand-by supply boats and fast rescue boats involved in the immediate rescue of survivors, and in the subsequent search for and recovery of bodies. Similarly, helicopter, police and medical personnel were on the scene quickly working in the most distressing of circumstances.

Additionally, the Piper platform was located in a position where it could be clearly seen by the men on three neighbouring locations, and the effects of such an event on the 'helpless witness' may emerge only months later. Similar contact victims were found at the football disasters at Bradford and Hillsborough.

People who 'might have been there' are also likely to come to the attention of a disaster team. Piper Alpha, like most oil rigs, worked a two week on, two week off shift system. This is known as a 'back to back' operation with each man on the rig having an opposite number on shore. Some of these men suffered quite traumatic reactions, as they came to appreciate the arbitrariness which seemed to decide that they should be safe, when in some cases they had been at work only hours before the platform disintegrated, killing the men who had replaced them.

These men were also contact victims in the much more direct sense that their place of work disappeared in the space of a few hours, leaving them without jobs and without an income.

Additionally, there were men who no longer worked on the Piper Alpha but had done so in the past. The North Sea oil population is not only transient but mobile and it is very much the exception for someone to work on only one platform. Most men move freely from one to another and almost all the North Sea oil workers lost personal friends on the Piper.

The office staff of the 29 companies who had men on board were contact victims. They lost friends and colleagues, as well as having to undertake distressing and unusual duties such as visiting the bereaved, returning personal belongings of the deceased to the next of kin, and trying to carry on.

The contact victims category will differ in every disaster but any social services team needs to be aware that they will exist and some effort needs to be made towards acknowledging their existence and encouraging them to make use of the help on offer. The Piper Outreach Team tried to reach people in this category through a variety of methods from the local media, to asking the companies to distribute literature to their employees, to GP's, Health Visitors to placing notices in libraries and Health Centres.

Peripheral victims

This category would encompass among others the family friends and employers of those event and contact victims. In a wider sense it could be said to affect entire communities and the village of Hungerford may well be a case in point.

The Peripheral Victim group was identified by Social Workers, dealing with the aftermath of the Herald of Free Enterprise sinking:

'people in the local area will face problems as a direct result of the loss of the ferry. Others, not actually on board the vessel at the time, but involved in the rescue attempts and salvage, or working for the company or relief agencies could find they are inexplicably unable to cope with the everyday stresses of work or family life. There could well be an increase in absenteeism from work through illness, and difficulties in personal relationships.'[3]

A similar reaction was noted by the leader of the Kings Cross Support Unit. Commenting on that disaster she stated:

'...thousands of people not directly involved were profoundly affected by it. There was a tremendous personal identification with this disaster. ...The people who died were not voyaging abroad or heading for somewhere exotic. They were commuting home from work for the most part. Thousands of people who just missed it or who commute regularly by tube watched the scenes on television that night and thought "My God, that could have been me." The habitual and the familiar had become the stuff of nightmares.'[4]

Entry victims

This category refers in the main to those people who do not live or work in the immediate vicinity of a disaster, but come into that area to lend their assistance, or because they have official functions to carry out as a result of the disaster.

Target groups

While this general model provides a useful overview, it is more important to identify specific target groups who provide the details on the model.

Following the Piper Alpha disaster, the social workers highlighted seven target groups to whom their services were to be offered. They were

1. Bereaved next of kin

2. Survivors - those on the platform at the time

3. Families/dependents of both these

4. Other Piper Alpha workers (those on opposite shift)

5. Other oil personnel

6. Rescue workers

7. Miscellaneous

'Other oil personnel' would cover everyone from receptionists in company offices to men on the neighbouring platform who watched the disaster unfolding. They both have distressing reactions but putting them into the same grouping may not take enough account of their differing circumstance. 'Rescue workers' would encompass men who in fast rescue boats put their own lives very much at risk and also policemen who, however distressing their task, certainly had a vastly different function and the category of 'rescue workers' may need some sub-division if it is to be helpful.

However, at this stage, the general model combined with identifiable target groups at least gives the disaster team some clearer idea of the people with whom they will be working, and can allow them to begin to develop appropriate strategies for approaching the different groups. The picture that is beginning to emerge can help to make some sense of what until then may have seemed like a disjointed jumbled welter of information, offers of help, requests for help, conflicting demands and needs. Having identified and to some extent prioritised the client groups, the first question to be addressed is the timing of the first approach.

Timing an approach

The pattern that has been followed in recent disasters is that letters of condolence or sympathy are sent out to those identified as bereaved or survivors as soon as possible. A follow-up letter advising that a visit will take place is sent within the next two weeks, and the high levels of acceptance suggest that this strategy and timing are about right.

There are two qualifications which do need to borne in mind. First, as concerns the bereaved, there is some evidence from the Piper Alpha response that the initial letters were not noticed. This could partly be explained by the fact that within a few days the next of kin are still too stunned to register the contents. Those who were asked for their views of the initial approach, months later, certainly had no recollection of receiving it. More likely, perhaps, is the possibility that the correspondence was just one among a welter of cards, notes and letters that people receive from family and friends at the time of a bereavement.

Second, as concerns the survivors of a major disaster, initial contact with them may be within a few days and the first visit within a few weeks. However, critical incident debriefing theory stresses the need for a first debriefing to take place within hours of the incident if physically and medically possible. Recalling the details and feelings of being involved is important and any significant time lapse allows the mind to move from recall to rationalisation.

The structure of social work help after a disaster may not allow for this but it is important for social workers dealing with survivors to realise this may not have taken place. Initial accounts of what happened by Piper Alpha survivors varied markedly not only as to what preceded the first explosion, but what occurred during the disaster, when it happened and how long events took to unfold.

At one survivors' group meeting after Piper Alpha, two survivors almost came to blows over their conflicting accounts of the same incident during the disaster.

The general rule of thumb over timing an approach would seem to be 'as soon as possible with the bereaved, but be aware it may not register, and the sooner the better in respect of survivors.'

Liaising with other agencies

One feature of post disaster work is that any central point established by social services will be inundated with offers of help. Not least amongst these will be offers from local voluntary organisations, who are often in a position to offer not only personnel to man helpline phones, but a great deal of experience and expertise.

There are many such organisations and while their strength may vary from one part of the country to another, most do have a national structure which can be invaluable where a disaster population is dispersed throughout the country.

Among the more prominent of such organisations are:

CRUSE

This organisation's main aim is to offer help and counselling to the bereaved. Their volunteer members are trained and experienced and were invaluable in the aftermath of Piper Alpha.

SAMARITANS

Their experience in dealing with people in major personal crisis is of obvious value, not only in the immediate aftermath of a disaster but in the longer term.

RED CROSS

Well known and well respected organisation. Their strength often lies in providing personnel and practical support. After the Herald of Free Enterprise sinking the Red Cross provided escort services and transport for both relatives and survivors on request.

COUNCILS OF SOCIAL SERVICE

Most major population centres will have a CSS or equivalent voluntary social services agency who will have trained and experienced personnel and often volunteers on whom they can call.

CHURCHES

The churches are usually among the first to offer help. Following the Piper Alpha disaster, church members offered to visit the bereaved, man the helpline service, and arranged accommodation for relatives visiting Aberdeen for the memorial service.

Keeping the representatives of all these voluntary organisations informed and involved in the post disaster work is crucially important. Knowing what help, expertise and experience is available and thus being able to deploy it effectively and efficiently can make the difference between offering meaningful assistance to people and an ineffective response.

People may also refer themselves directly to one of these agencies either immediately or in the months following a disaster and developing good initial links can help to maintain a clear picture of who is offering what help to whom.

Computer/database systems

Although not the most exciting of subjects, the establishment of an effective information recording or data-base system is one of the most important. If accurate, easily accessible records are not established and maintained then it becomes impossible to offer help. This message comes over loud and clear from all recent post disaster work. The report into the *Herald of Free Enterprise* sinking highlights the point.

'The Common Information System was seen as central to the management of the welfare agencies' responses. It was expected that the co-ordination and dissemination of information would allow for the targetting of appropriate assistance to all those affected by the disaster. Enlarged data base facilities and a more sophisticated programme became necessary as the amount of relevant information in use, continues to be used by all welfare agencies.

It has been hoped that the existing information relating to people resident outside the County of Kent could be made available through the Directors of Social Services throughout the country so that they could plan their response, relay information, make enquiries and ask for assistance from the Unit.

The database will hopefully help in the co-ordination of the many offers of help from voluntary organisations and individuals.'[5]

The message was the same from Bradford. Compile a good data- base early and keep it updated, and you have a solid foundation on which to build any offer of help or support.

The people who established the Dover data-base travelled to Aberdeen after Piper Alpha and advised on the most appropriate systems and programmes.

Records and confidentiality

The perennial disquiet that social workers often feel about keeping computerised files on people can be heightened in disaster work.

When social workers offer their services in the pro-active way previously described, the morality of keeping computerised social work files on those who accept the offer of help is at least questionable. 'What will you be writing about me' and ' who will see it' were not questions universally raised after Piper Alpha, but they were asked by a significant number of people. In any event, simply not raising the question does not mean it is not valid to pose it.

Assuring people that the records principally consisted of personal information, relationships and what kind of assistance was being received and from whom seemed to allay most fears. Offering to show, and actually showing on request, people the information held on them also helped.

Access to records was strictly controlled. Grampian Region operates a main-frame computer system throughout its area. Piper Alpha clients would appear on this, listed by name and address and the contact of Piper Alpha. The more detailed personal records were held on a separate micro computer in the Piper Outreach office accessible only by team members.

This combination of strategies seemed the best way to allay fears, guarantee confidentiality and at the same time keep the necessary information readily available to allow the social workers to offer effective help based on reliable information.

Points for discussion

1. Consider the problems connected with identifying a disaster population following a major train crash involving large numbers of both deceased and survivors.

2. In a disaster situation where there are a large number of witnesses - eg a football ground - what strategies might be useful in attempting to encourage them to seek help?

3. Apart from the voluntary agencies mentioned in this chapter, who else might it be important for Social Services to liaise with after a disaster?

4. Consider the problems, both practical and ethical, of speedily establishing a computer data-base following a major disaster.

References

1. Raphael, Beverley (1986). *When Disaster Strikes*. Hutchinson.
2. Bradford City Fire Disaster: Social Services Response. Information Pack (P.4). Bradford City Council. November, 1987.
3. *Herald of Free Enterprise* Disaster - Dover Harbour, 001. Dover City Council. March 1987.
4. One Short Chaotic Year. *Community Care*, 1988.
5. *Herald of Free Enterprise* Disaster - Dover Harbour, 012. *op. cit.*

Chapter 4

Coping with significant events

It is recognised that the process of grieving includes various responses on the part of the bereaved which, although they can be set out as stages, actually form a continuum along which a bereaved person may regress as well as progress.

The highlights on this continuum might be, as categorised by Bowlby,[1] an initial denial and disbelief, then anger, weeping, fear and panic, then despair and hopelessness and finally restoration and acceptance. A bereaved person might not move smoothly from one stage to the next at a set time scale, but can get stuck at points along the way and may regress in certain conditions. Part of the work of the counsellor is to recognise this and help the grieving person through.

This issue will be addressed more fully in chapter 9, but in working with loss it is important to understand, and have an appreciation of, the phases of bereavement.

These phases would apply generally in cases of bereavement but the circumstances of the loss may cause a heightening or sharpening of the reaction, or introduce additional elements.

The loss of a young child may cause the parents and siblings to have acute feelings of guilt, while a sudden or unexpected loss may also cause guilt resulting from things being left unresolved, as well as fear in what now seems an unsafe and unpredictable world.

The reactions of a support group established to help those bereaved by or wounded in two mass shooting incidents in Melbourne Australia in 1987 illustrate the point:

'Shock and disbelief followed by preoccupation with the event, a need to speak of the loss repeatedly in an attempt to increase its reality, and then expressions of anger, sadness, guilt and fear and a compulsion to find meaning, and ask why, searching for answers. Physical sensations such as heart palpitations, insomnia and lack of energy were also reported ... [also] ... disillusionment about the world in general and fears about personal safety were expressed. Anger was directed at television crews who filmed a dead man slumped over the wheel of his car announcing his death to his family in a brutally public way.'[2]

Following a bereavement, and especially in the first year after the loss, critical times and significant events will occur of which the counsellor or social worker needs to be aware. Anticipating them and discussing them with the bereaved person can help them to cope and this was confirmed by a young widowed mother who said 'thinking through Christmas before it occurred definitely helped me.'[3]

Christmas is one obvious time when a bereaved person might find things especially difficult, but it is only one of a number of what Lundin categorised as 'anniversary reactions'.

> All that happens regularly each year will be compared, on a preconscious and conscious level, with the same situations earlier in life. This might be the explanation of the change in quality of the grief reaction after the first year.[4]

Ten such significant times or events can be identified which may cause the bereaved person particular difficulties with all sorts of thoughts, feelings and emotions jumbled together and at which times they may need extra support.

1. Funeral service

A very important part of the grieving process which allows the bereaved to say good-bye to the deceased in a ritually accepted form. Religious beliefs can assist a bereaved person here as they can help introduce a sense of meaning into events which may otherwise appear devoid of meaning. The funeral is normally a time at which family and friends 'rally round' to offer the bereaved additional support and comfort.

2. Memorial service

Where a funeral is restricted to immediate family, it is not uncommon for a memorial service to be arranged subsequently for friends, work colleagues and others to pay their respects to the deceased. For the bereaved it becomes another occasion at which thoughts of the deceased and the loss are vividly recalled.

3. Deceased's birthday

Particularly the first diseased's birthday following death can be a very difficult time. Thoughts of the deceased's last birthday, of gifts given, are bound to be stressful and distressing to the bereaved. It is also an event which will not be widely acknowledged by others outside very close family.

4. Surviving partner's birthday

The surviving partner's birthday is likely to be difficult for the same reasons as the deceased's. Normally a time for gifts and celebration will be replaced by sadness at being alone and intensified by memories of the last shared birthday.

5. Wedding anniversary

The wedding anniversary is, again, a time now divested of previous celebration. Memories of both the last anniversary and of the wedding itself can make the first anniversary following the death a particularly difficult time.

6. Children's birthdays

Children's birthdays are probably among the most difficult times for surviving partners. There can be no more physical reminder of a dead person than his or her children, and their birthdays have special significance. The bereaved often try to make special efforts at celebration 'for the children's sake', but it is difficult to do that with commitment, and unlikely that the children, unless infants, will feel celebratory.

7. Christmas/New Year

Like birthdays, Christmas and New Year are times associated with celebration and gift giving, the difference being that they are public celebrations. The emphasis through television, churches, shops and the press of this being a time for family gatherings, new beginnings and moving into a new year can make it a particularly stressful time for someone recently bereaved. Added to that public celebration of family is the memory of the last Christmas and New Year spent with the deceased.

This is one of the critical times in the year following a bereavement when the wider family may be expected to offer extra support. After Piper Alpha a number of those bereaved commented that Christmas was not as bad as they had been anticipating, but that New Year was much worse. Offers from the wider family for the bereaved and children to spend Christmas with them, combined with the anticipation of it as a potentially difficult time, clearly did help. Less overt support was offered for the New Year period and they were largely confronted on their own with the passing of the year in which their partner had died, and entering one which he would not share with them. Sadness and grieving can be deepened by isolation, particularly at a time of public celebration.

8. Personally significant times

Most relationships will have their own personally significant times, which may be known only to the partners. These could include the anniversary of their first meeting, of their engagement or any of the other very personal times and events which are part of any relationship. The bereaved is less likely to share this information, but such a time may account for an increase in stress or sadness.

9. Anniversary

The first anniversary of a death is an obvious time when someone bereaved may find difficulty in coping and when a counsellor can play a valuable role both in acknowledging the need and in physically being in contact. Depending on the circumstances of the death, the main time of distress may not coincide with the exact date of the anniversary but the period around it. After the Piper Alpha disaster, which happened on 6th July, one widow commented that it was harder for her to 'get through the 3rd than the 6th, because he left to go off-shore on the 3rd. It was the last time I saw him.'

10. Anniversary of the funeral

While the first anniversary of someone's death is acknowledged as being difficult, the anniversary of the funeral tends to be forgotten, other than by the bereaved. As the funeral provides the ritualised process of saying farewell and is the focus for so much grief, its first anniversary is unlikely to pass without effect on the surviving partner.

This post-bereavement calendar applies to the surviving partner of a marriage or relationship. With some adjustments a very similar calendar would be constructed which would be applicable to a parent losing a child, a child losing a parent or a sibling losing a brother or sister.

The first year following a bereavement seems to be a particularly difficult time for a grieving partner or relative. Memories and emotions are fresh and raw and the year is peppered with significant events, some or all of which are liable to act as trigger mechanisms focusing a bereaved person's grief in a sharp and distressing manner.

Following a major disaster, those bereaved by it will have this personal calendar to go through, but additionally they will have to cope with the public calendar which follows on from a public tragedy.

Looking back on the year which followed the Kings Cross Tube disaster the social worker responsible for co-ordinating the social service team acknowledged the centrality of this public calendar to their work:

> 'It's been a short chaotic year for all involved with the inquest, the Fennell Inquiry report, the recent coverage of the anniversary of the fire, all coming close on each other's heels.'[5]

Again, those working in the aftermath of the Herald of Free Enterprise sinking were able to identify parts of this public scenario which would provide opportunities for useful intervention.

> 'It is possible, and we should be able to offer good anticipatory responses across a range of activities. For example, on issues concerning
>
> · returning the bodies home

· assisting the coroner
· righting the ship
· identification
· the ship as a grave
⸫ where people actually died
· memorial service
· progress of the appeal

These are all tasks which provide opportunities to help and prevent further hurt.'[6]

The public calendar of significant events following a disaster does provide an opportunity which those involved in helping can anticipate and ensure that support is being offered. The real significance of these events, and one way in which disaster victims are different to others bereaved by sudden death, is the public setting for the bereaved's private grief.

Following the Piper Alpha oil rig disaster these significant events stretched throughout the year and were all highlighted on TV, radio, in the local and national press and in magazines. There was little chance of the bereaved avoiding the constantly repeated pictures, video film and banner headlines, even if they wished to do so. Also, a cause of great distress was the feeling that their private, personal loss was a thing of the public domain, packaged and presented to sell newspapers with little or no concern for their or their children's feelings.

The public events on the calendar following the Piper Alpha disaster included the following:

· Initial body recovery
· Public Memorial Service
· Disaster Fund establishment
· Companies Memorial Services
· Recovery of accommodation quarters
· TV documentaries
· Body recovery from accommodation module
· Funerals of those recovered
· Public Inquiry opening
· Police evidence - causes of death, where bodies were found, means
  of identification
· Survivors' evidence to Inquiry
· Destruction of remains of Piper Alpha by explosion
· Anniversary Memorial Service

- · Journey to Piper Alpha site for relatives
- · Production of Inquiry Report
- · Compensation settlements

All of these events, with the exception of the last two, took place within the twelve months following the disaster. All of them were events which seemed, to some of the bereaved, almost designed to keep their grief and loss at the front of their minds and in the full public gaze. Nor were all these events of a one-off or short term duration.

The disaster fund, like others established before it, was set up to allow the public a way of expressing their concern and of helping those affected. Also like others before it, it gave rise to disputes, acrimony and a degree of distress over a period of months that no-one wanted or anticipated.

Similarly, the Public Inquiry, designed to find out the facts behind the disaster came for some relatives to be a physically and emotionally draining experience in which the participants seemed almost remote and off-hand when discussing their dead relative. The very thoroughness with which the Inquiry addressed the workings of an oil platform to try and determine the cause of the disaster often seemed irrelevant to the bereaved overwhelmed by the results of it.

The Public Inquiry started six months after the disaster and sat almost daily for a year following.

Being aware that those bereaved in a major disaster will have both a private and a public calendar for the year following the event and beyond, can enable social workers to anticipate when extra support may be welcomed. It should also help them understand why those bereaved in a disaster may not move through the grieving process uninterruptedly and may be more liable to regression then expected.

One thing which may adversely affect those bereaved in a disaster which cannot be anticipated is the effect of subsequent disasters. The year following the Piper Alpha tragedy saw the Ocean Odyssey oil rig explosion, the Lockerbie Disaster, the Hillsborough Football ground disaster and the Marchioness pleasure boat sinking. Significant numbers of both bereaved and survivors of Piper Alpha reported being affected by news of these tragedies in a much more personal and powerful way than they had previously been. Having gone through it themselves they knew what was beginning to unfold for those involved as well as being vividly reminded of the early days after Piper Alpha.

Example - Calendar of Mrs B's significant events

Mrs B was married for ten years and has two children aged eight and six. Her husband had worked on the Piper Alpha for four years prior to the disaster. His body was not recovered immediately following the explosions but some four months later when the main accommodation module was recovered from the sea-bed, and taken to the shore.

The following calendar shows the significant events of one widow bereaved by the Piper Alpha disaster.

	Private	Public
July 1988	Husband's death	Massive media coverage Memorial service Disaster Fund established
Aug 1988	Youngest child's birthday	Husband's company holds memorial for all employees lost on Piper Alpha Disaster Fund row goes on
Sept 1988		TV documentary on 'Cost of Oil' including film of Piper Alpha Ocean Odyssey Rig fire - one dead, 66 rescued. Media comparisons with Piper
Oct 1988	Husband's body found returned in sealed coffin Funeral Service	Module - body recovery and identification
Nov 1988	Husband's birthday Oldest child's birthday	Stories of compensation offers in newspapers
Dec 1988	Christmas/New Year	Lockerbie Disaster - Media comparisons and coverage of 'Year of the Disaster'
Jan 1989		Public Inquiry opens Massive press coverage

Feb 1989	Mrs B's birthday	Police evidence to Inquiry re cause of death, location of body and means of ID video of disaster shown for first time. Survivors begin evidence
March 1989		Survivors evidence to Inquiry continues Remains of Piper Alpha Rig toppled by explosion
April 1989	Wedding Anniversary	Hillsborough Disaster
May 1989		Public Inquiry resumes after Easter break
June 1989	Anniversary of Mr B leaving home to go off-shore	
July 1989	Anniversary of husband's death Boat trip to Piper Alpha site	Anniversary of Disaster with attendant media coverage Public Memorial Service

While both the public, and to a lesser extent the private, calendar will vary from one individual to another and depend on the nature of the disaster, the principle of these two series of post disaster timetables working in tandem show why those bereaved in a disaster may find it more difficult to arrive at 'restoration and acceptance'. Being aware of these events can allow a social worker to offer effective support at appropriate times.

Points for discussion

1. Consider what other events, or times, of both a private and public nature may cause difficulty for the bereaved in the year following a disaster.
2. What problems could be anticipated in trying to establish a calendar of significant events in a post disaster situation?
3. In what ways would such a timetable of significant events differ if extended into the second year following a disaster?

4. Consider the ways in which a social worker might help a bereaved person with the grieving process in the period following such tragedy, and how he might overcome the problems of a public calendar.

References

1. Bowlby, J., (1961). Process in Mourning. *Journal of Psycho Analysis*.
2. After the Shootings: Disaster Recovery in Melbourne, Australia. Irene Renzenbrint. Paper presented at 'International Conference on Grief and Bereavement in Contemporary Society'. London. July 1988.
3. Worden, (1982). *Grief Counselling and Grief Therapy*. Tavistock Publications.
4. Lundin, Tom, (1987). The Stress of Unexpected Bereavement. *Psychology of Stress: Stress Medicine*. Vol.3. 1987. John Wiley. London.
5. One Short Chaotic Year - Kings Cross Fire. *Community Care*. 1988.
6. *Herald of Free Enterprise* disaster. Dover Harbour, 010, *op. cit.*

Chapter 5

Case studies of people bereaved

Introduction

This chapter looks at case studies of two women bereaved by the Piper Alpha disaster of July 1988. In both cases the women's names, the names of the men who died, and other family members names have been changed to protect their anonymity.

Both women kept daily diaries, one for a week and one for a fortnight, which show their living routines 13 months after their bereavement. These diaries are reproduced in diagrammatic form, using social network analysis and are also commented upon.[1]

Both women were subsequently interviewed in September 1989 and reflect on their feelings and how they both coped with their grief over this period. They also reflect on the help offered to them in their bereavement, what they found helpful and what they found less so.

Case Study 1: Mrs Mary Banks

Mrs Banks is a married lady in her mid-fifties. She and her husband had three sons. The oldest is married with a family of his own. The second son John, aged 25, lived at home but was due to become engaged to Joyce, his girlfriend. The youngest son also lives at home. Mrs Banks is employed as a nurse in a local hospital. John was employed by a company specialising in the cleaning of specialist engineering equipment and the company were often contracted by oil companies to carry out this function on their off-shore installations. In mid 1988 the company were under contract to carry out this work on the Piper Alpha platform, 120 miles off the coast of Aberdeen. John was on his two week tour of duty on July 6th 1988 when the platform was devastated by a series of explosions and consumed in fire. Following the disaster, 167 of the 230 men on board the platform died. John Banks was one of them and he is one of the 30 men whose body has never been recovered from the North Sea.

Mrs Banks was known to social workers soon after the disaster, but did not choose to use the services offered initially. After the opening of the Public Inquiry in January 1989 she became more involved. Following the formation of the Piper Alpha Families and Survivors Association she became centrally involved in their various campaigns and activities, especially the attempt to raise £100,000 for a permanent memorial. The following interview took place with Mrs Banks in September 1989, some fourteen months after the disaster.

Interview with Mrs. Banks.

DT Who did you turn to immediately after the disaster happened, for help or comfort?

MB Close family. A lot of friends of John came round. Joyce - John's girlfriend - and her family. Lots of people.

DT You have carried on working in your job as a nurse virtually throughout. How did you manage this and how did that feel?

MB The Senior Nursing Officer came to see me and told me to take off whatever time I wanted. Some colleagues visited. I took a few weeks off at the time. We went to see some relatives in Glasgow and a very old friend in England. We came back for the Memorial Service, and then some friends came to visit from abroad. After that, it got awfully quiet. I couldn't cope with being in the house. I spent a lot of time in John's room, looking through photos.

I decided to go back to work but asked that people should not speak about it.

I managed to cope with the patients OK, a lot of them are elderly.

I didn't feel any anger towards them although some of the ones who had been abusing alcohol were difficult. They would get palpitations and say they were dying. I found it hard to be sympathetic to them. But I managed to keep things separate. That's how I coped.

DT When you first got a letter from a social worker and a visit, what did you think?

MB I don't remember getting a letter. Everything was dazed. The first I remember was I got a card from A (the social worker) saying she would call round and I thought, what do I need a social worker for? They deal with the homeless and down and outs, people with social problems - what's that got to do with me? When she first came, I had a call from a friend asking if I would see R (another mother whose son had died on Piper Alpha), and her car arrived just after A came, so I asked if she could come back and she did, a week or so later.

All I wanted to do was to talk about the bitterness and anger I felt towards the [main] company and John's company too. He hadn't wanted to go. He was worried about something. At that time nobody knew the cause of the accident and I just knew he worked with dangerous chemicals and hadn't wanted to go. He told me about a briefing he'd had from the company that worried him. You remember all this stuff.

DT   You first seemed to get involved publicly at the time of the Inquiry. Why then? What motivated you?

MB   For months everything was building up and building up inside. I used to speak to John, and write poetry about him. I decided to get involved publicly because I wanted justice for John and to help me as well.

When John's body was not recovered, I was devastated. Before, we had always had someone in the house waiting for the Police to call. When he was not recovered my imagination was going crazy. I know from my job a little about decomposition and I was crazy.

It was around the time they brought up the module that I thought I must get involved for John's sake.

DT   From then, through the Piper Alpha Families Association, you have been quite closely involved with the social workers of the Piper Outreach Team. What, if any, benefits have you derived from the contact?

MB   The Families Association has been very helpful because of the circumstances of the Piper. It's not like a car accident where you have a body and can bury or cremate it.

Not knowing what happened and not getting John back meant that the Families Association let you cling to other people who have gone through the same. The worst thing in the world is for your children to pre-decease you.

As a nurse I often had to deal with bereavement, but now I realise I didn't know what it's like at all. You think you do, but you don't.

We used to have a busy social life with parties and barbecues but now it's nearly nil. Everything now is Piper Alpha. Anything else seems to be too trivial.

DT   You got together with others around the time of the forming of the Families Association at the start of the Public Inquiry in January. Would it have helped to get together sooner?

MB   Well, it's hard to say. It might have been useful to get together around the time they raised the [accommodation] module. I'm not sure about before that.

DT   What criticisms would you make of the social work help available?

MB   None really. They couldn't have offered help any sooner. As I said before, my idea of a social worker was haywire. The Piper Outreach Team could not have done more, helping us with what we had to go through.

DT   Who or what was the single most helpful person or thing to you since the disaster?

MB   First of all my close family. Not so much my husband. That sounds strange but I couldn't deal with his grief and I don't suppose he could deal with mine. But my sister and also Joyce, John's girlfriend. After that the Piper Outreach Team were the most helpful.

DT   Where do you see yourself a year from now?

MB   A year from now. The memorial is very important for me. I hope I'm still working. Also to keep on with the Piper Alpha Families Association, and the connection between everybody. It should not be forgotten. In a year or two my husband should be retired, and I hope we can get a little cottage on the West Coast. I'd like to write, I've always tried little bits. Not about the Piper Alpha, although it may be. Well, that's in the future.

Diary : Mrs Mary Banks.

Figure 3 shows a week of activities in Mrs Banks' life some 15 months after her son was killed. It represents a fairly normal week, dominated by her demanding job at the local hospital and by household chores. She keeps work days and the days when she attends the Piper office separate, as far as possible.

It can be noted that as well as keeping in touch with things through the Piper Outreach social workers and the Piper Families Association, she is still in contact with her late son's girlfriend and her parents.

Mrs Banks acknowledged in her interview the important role Joyce had played in supporting and helping her in her grief. This was reciprocated with Joyce acknowledging the help she had received from Mrs Banks.

This was not always the case with similar relationships. Most of the men who died on Piper Alpha were relatively young and significant numbers were recently married or about to be married.

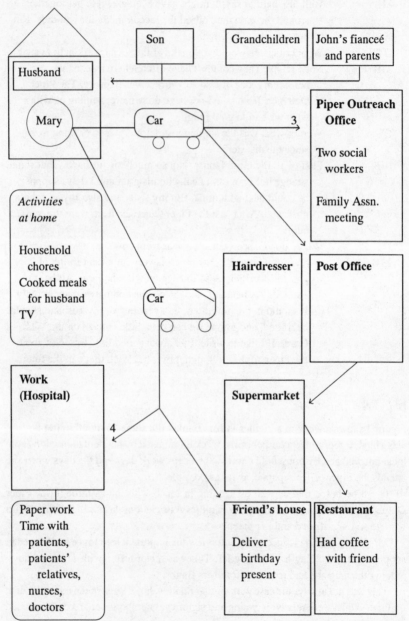

*Figure 3 - A week in Mary Bank's life, 15 months after the disaster
(for explanation of symbols, see key, page 114)*

Where they were in fairly new relationships like this, it was not uncommon for the bereaved parents and the bereaved fiancee or widow to become intensely rivalrous.

This rivalry is understandable in the sense that the parents had only recently seen their son enter a new relationship and still felt him to be physically part of their family. The new wife felt him to be her husband primarily and his parents' son only after that. When these differing viewpoints could not be reconciled, rivalry was often the result.

This was not the case with Mrs Banks and Joyce who constantly offered each other mutual support for over a year after their loss.

It is worth commenting on the extent to which Mrs Banks' coping strategy was successful. She maintained that she managed to carry out her nursing duties much as before. She used the social workers' office to talk openly and honestly about her hurt and bitterness and would often become tearful and upset while there. She felt that that safety valve, as it were, helped her maintain her coping appearance elsewhere.

Case Study 2: Miss Patricia Murdoch

Patricia is in her late twenties and was engaged to be married to her fiancee, Bill Hughes, in 1989. He was employed by a small specialist firm offering services to the oil industry. She works as a secretary in an employment agency specialising in recruitment for the off-shore oil and gas industry.

Bill's job rarely required him to go off-shore but he was working on the Piper Alpha platform on July 6th 1988 and died in the explosion. His body was not recovered immediately. When the accommodation module was raised from the sea-bed and brought to shore, his was one of the bodies removed from it, and he was subsequently buried in Aberdeen.

Patricia continued working for some time after the disaster but eventually, unable to cope, she gave up. She became very involved in the development of the Piper Alpha Families and Survivors Association and particularly in the campaign to raise the necessary finance to erect a permanent memorial to the 167 men who died that night. As time went on, this became her primary focus. As well as her personal commitment she brought her considerable organisational and administrative skills to this task.

She is a regular user of the Piper Outreach office and finds no difficulty in seeking help or advice from the social workers there when necessary. She did not do so initially, although she was aware of the offer and did receive a visit from a social worker soon after the disaster. She subsequently was referred to the Piper Outreach Team by her GP

She gave the following interview in September 1989.

Interview with Miss Patricia Murdoch

DT	Who did you turn to for comfort and support immediately after the disaster happened?
PM	Bill's parents. Also Alice, a female friend of 17 years standing. Also a couple of Bill's friends.
DT	You carried on working for about six months after the disaster happened. How did that feel and how did you manage?
PM	I took three weeks off immediately after it happened, and another two when Bill's body was found. Apart from that I kept on going to work. I hated it, but people encouraged me to keep working. It would do me good, they told me.
	Everyday I was hearing about oil, and typing things often that had to do with the Piper. Reports, CV's of people who'd been on the Piper. The problem was the close connection between the job and the oil industry. A job that had nothing to do with oil might have been helpful in taking my mind off it, but I couldn't get away from it.
DT	When you got a letter and subsequent visit from a social worker, what did you think?
PM	I don't really remember the letter. I think my GP referred me. I remember C (the social worker) came for about one hour. She gave some general background and asked if I was experiencing peculiar feelings and sensations. She said others were, and that helped.
	She said she would not be contacting me all the time but was there, if and when I needed. I didn't keep contact at that time as I had just so much to do. No time. I got back in touch with the Outreach Team in October, looking for information. When the module came up I wanted information from the police and so on, and thought I can't do that. So I was really looking for help to get information in here. [Outreach Office]
DT	After you stopped working, what plans, if any, did you have?
PM	The office routine changed. They brought in new computer systems and we had to sit day after day watching this woman show us how they worked. I thought I understood, but one day I went back to try on my own and I didn't know a thing. I couldn't cope. I just couldn't cope, wasn't interested. On the day I finished, I was hysterical. I wouldn't have gone back if you'd given me a million pounds. I couldn't have done it. I didn't care. I was initially signed off with depression for a

month and I thought I'd go back to work then, but it didn't work out.

It was New Year before I had time to miss Bill. For four months I couldn't give in. I had to keep going. I had a series of targets and just strived for each one, like the bringing up of the module, the Public Inquiry. I couldn't let myself go. Not give in.

DT   What brought you to the Piper Outreach Team?

PM   As I said before, initially looking for information.

DT   What, if any, benefit have you derived from your contact with the social workers of the Piper Outreach Team?

PM   I started to feel really guilty about talking about the Piper after six months or so. People, even friends, were getting bored.

The best thing about here [Outreach Office] was knowing it was safe to talk or not talk about it. It's a safe environment.

I also met so many people here who had a connection with Piper Alpha, but not just so you could be sad. It also made it possible to be able to laugh safely, without people thinking 'she shouldn't be laughing' or whatever.

Also, you can get information and help here even about non-Piper things. If you're having a bad time you can just say 'Oh, can you go over the road and pay my electric bill, I'm not up to it.'

But also information from the police or about the Inquiry. It's not dependency because when you need it, at a really bad point, you've been here. It's knowing you're here when you need it.

DT   What, with hindsight, would you have found helpful to you in the first few months? 1) Professional help, 2) Contact with others on an individual basis, 3) Group contact, 4) Other

PM   The way things happened, that is gradually, was best for me. Meeting people earlier or being asked to groups wouldn't have helped. Professional help wouldn't have meant much to me and I wouldn't have been ready. I was too busy.

DT   What criticisms, if any, would you make of the social work help made available?

PM   No real criticism. It was good when C came, to just have someone to talk to. It was good she said 'we're here if you want, we'll not phone every day, but will come when you want.'

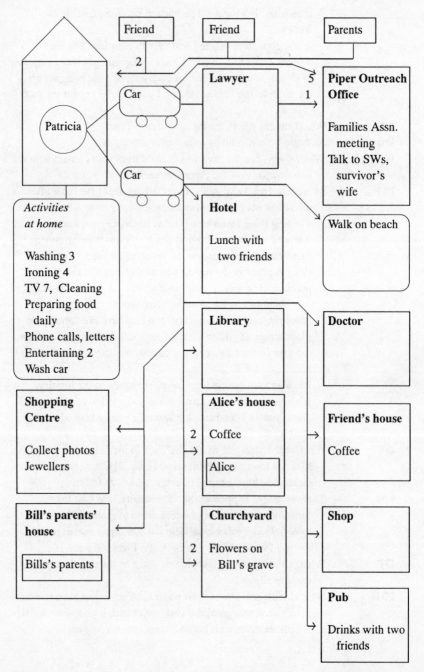

Figure 4 - A fortnight in Patricia Murdoch's life, 13 months after the disaster

DT	What has been the single most helpful thing or person to you since last July?
PM	Number one, my friend Alice. Number two, getting to know Susan (another fiancée bereaved by Piper Alpha).
DT	Where do you see yourself a year from now?
PM	First, still working on the memorial. Perhaps helping to set up and run a Families Association office, to keep things going after the social workers have gone. Then, perhaps getting another job.

Diary : Miss Patricia Murdoch.

Patricia kept a daily diary of activities over a two week period in August of 1989, some thirteen months after the disaster (Figure 4). By the time of keeping the diary, Patricia had given up her employment and this lack of work centre contrasts with the centrality of the hospital workplace in Mrs Banks' diary.

The two obvious differences between these representations and those of Mrs Banks are Patricia's more frequent use of the Piper Outreach Office, and her visits to the grave of her fiancé. Mrs Banks was denied that routine or element of comfort as her son's body was not recovered.

With the absence of employment it can be seen that the Piper Outreach Office had become the central focus for Patricia after home. She called in at the office on six of the ten days it was open.

In addition some of the phone calls and letter writing noted as 'activities at home' were connected with the work of the Piper Alpha Families and Survivors Association. The visits to the social work office varied from dropping in for an hour and having a snack lunch with the social workers, to an entire afternoon, to a three and a half hour evening meeting of the Families Association.

Two visits to her fiancé's grave to put fresh flowers down and a visit to his parents are also features of note, and the continuing involvement of, and support by, numerous friends are seen to be an important feature of Patricia's life.

Points for discussion

1. Compare the coping strategies of Mrs Banks and Miss Murdoch as shown in their diaries and interviews. What are their special strengths and weaknesses?

2. What part did work play in the aftermath of the disaster for Mrs Banks and for Mrs Murdoch? How would you respond to the issues about work which each case raises?

3. Mrs Banks was supported by Joyce, John's girlfriend. Discuss the comment that in other cases 'it was not uncommon for the bereaved parents and the bereaved fiancée

or widow to become intensely rivalrous.' How would you help the bereaved to handle such feelings?

4. Consider Mrs Banks' feelings about John's body not being recovered. How would you help her to cope with her feelings?

5. Discuss the value of the contacts with the outreach social work office for these two clients.

6. It could be argued that creating a special disaster team after a major accident could be detrimental to the bereaved in that it could prevent them from 'moving on'. Is there any evidence to support this view from the two case studies?

Reference

1. Seed, P. (1990) *Introducing network analysis in social work*. London: Jessica Kingsley.

Chapter 6

Questionnaire to people bereaved

A questionnaire was sent to 91 people bereaved by the Piper Alpha disaster. This was sent in August 1989, thirteen months after the disaster. Its distribution was restricted to those in the Grampian area, covered by the Piper Outreach Team. This allowed an element of control as the social workers were aware of what had been offered to the bereaved in the way of counselling, group-based work and informal contacts.

The questionnaires were designed to try to elicit from the bereaved what they had found useful following the disaster, and what they had found less so. It was not intended to have any purpose beyond providing a view of social work strategies in the wake of a disaster, from the point of view of those bereaved.

The findings are discussed question by question. A final section deals with the general comments people chose to make.

Of the 91 people who received the questionnaire 45 completed and returned it to the Piper Outreach Office.

In the disaster, did you lose a partner/son/brother/father?	
a) Partner	24
b) Son	18
c) Brother	-
d) Father	3
Total	45

One respondent indicated that she was separated from her partner prior to the disaster. Another crossed out partner very firmly, and wrote 'husband'.

Since the disaster have you had contact with other bereaved regularly/occasionally/not at all?			
	Regularly	*Occasionally*	*Not at all*
a) Lost partner	10	13	1
b) Lost son	4	11	3
c) Lost father	-	1	2
Totals	14	25	6

If so, was this helpful?			
	Yes	No	Other
a) Lost partner	18	3	2
b) Lost son	15	-	-
c) Lost father	1	-	-
Totals	34	3	2

Of the two in the 'other' category, one recorded no answer to the question and one said, 'At first, it was most helpful but as time went on, I found meeting these people very depressing.'

If you have met with others in groups, were these organised by social workers/company/church/other?	
a) Social workers	31
b) Company	3
c) Church	3
d) Other	2
Total	39

Some people who used groups attended more than one, and so multiple responses are included here.

People attending groups were asked if they had any comments. Of the 39 respondents who attended groups, 23 chose to make comments. Twenty commented favourably, most recording comments like 'helpful', 'supportive', etc. Some of the fuller statements are recorded below.

1. 'Found it helpful to talk to others at coffee mornings and widows' groups. G and R (social workers) I feel were very good and always made me feel better for having spoken with them.'

2. 'Having a social worker present initially helped to start up conversations until the bereaved knew each other sufficiently to feel comfortable with each other.'

3. 'Yes, I have met with others through my husband's company, but I feel, personally, that my meetings with some of the other bereaved families, through the social work department, have been of great help to me, in seeing how other wives and families are coping with the hurdles we had to cross and just being able to talk to someone in my situation.'

4. 'Most helpful was to realise you are not on your own, that others were facing the same or similar difficulties. The social workers in attendance at the meetings were really helpful making sure that everyone was included and helped if needed.'

5. 'I did not find these helpful because I felt I had enough problems without listening to others whose lives were as bad as mine - I found this a bit negative. I needed a more positive outlook on life as there is a lot of it ahead.'

6. I feel if it wasn't for the social workers, I would have taken a lot longer to face what happened. They helped bring families together, we found hidden strength within each other, when faced with the fact that we can never have a funeral or even a grave for our loved ones.'

7. 'I found the meetings very helpful and I'm glad I went but as time went on, I felt I did not want to be always talking about the disaster. I wanted to get on with my life and make the best of what was left.'

8. 'Apart from the Piper Outreach Team, the companies involved or the Church paid no attention to the needs of the parents.'

9. 'I didn't enjoy the group meetings, but a lot of the wives got comfort from them.'

10. 'A tower of strength in gaining self-confidence and facing life and the outside world again, patient, understanding and so dependable, giving a strong feeling of security to re-adjust without my son.'

11. 'Although the oil company initiated the original meeting of bereaved which proved successful, a feeling of discomfort and resentment towards "them" developed later. Meetings organised through the Outreach Team had a more relaxed, sincere feel to them. It was quite surprising how many people managed top overcome their natural inhibitions and share with the social workers in an honest, open way.'

Have you seen any of the following since the disaster?	
a) GP (other than for minor ailments)	24
b) Psychiatrist/psychologist (How often, approx.?)	2
c) Social worker (How often, approx.?)	29
d) Other professional (How often, approx.?)	6

Of those seeing GPs or social workers on a regular basis the average was once per month to GPs and once per fortnight for social workers. The 'other professionals' category included one community psychiatric nurse, two health visitors, two vicars/ministers, and one counsellor.

The frequency of visits to GPs ranged from one-off to once per week. Frequency of social work visits was from twice in the year to one respondent who wrote, 'daily (!)'

Social work in the wake of disaster

> **In so far as possible could you indicate which of the following has been most helpful to you since the disaster.**
>
> a) Family, b) Minister, c) Friends, d) Other bereaved,
> e) Professionals (if so which),
> f) Others (please specify)

All 45 respondents chose to answer this question, and many made multiple choices, some even listing them from 1-6. The total results are recorded here.

a)	Family	33
b)	Minister/Vicar	12
c)	Friends	24
d)	Other bereaved	7
e)	Professionals	23
f)	Others	4

Of the 23 listing 'professionals' 20 stated social worker, two recorded Health Visitor and one recorded Community Psychiatrist Nurse.

Of the four stating others one registered 'neighbours', one 'Counsellor', one 'Teachers' and one recorded 'self' adding 'I found I had to live for myself before I was any good to my children, or my parents-in-law, or to friends.'

> **Is there any particular thing you would have found helpful in the year following the disaster, but which was not offered?**
>
> | | |
> |---|---|
> | No entry recorded | 21 |
> | Answered 'No' or equivalent | 13 |
> | Stated that everything possible had been offered | 3 |
> | Specific requests or complaints (These are recorded below) | 8 |

---

1. 'An acknowledgement from the employing company of my loss, plus more information at an early stage about how he died.' - *from a parent.*

2. 'My husband was one of the people who was not found till five months later. I would have found it helpful to have been given regular bulletins as to how the progress of finding bodies etc. were doing. I was kept very much in the dark from start to finish.' - *from a wife.*

3. 'I personally think that the widows, who like myself are genuinely grieving, could have been saved the embarrassment of doctors failing to understand if the team had dealt with stress on a better level.' - *from a wife.*

4. 1) 'My father's employers could have made more of an effort to keep in touch with the family from time to time.'
   2) '*No* correspondence at all from Occidental (the owners of Piper Alpha) at any time during or after the disaster.' - *from a son.*

5. 'Time on your own to think things out for yourself without 'do-gooders' trying to advise!! I know this worked for me, but, obviously not for the majority.' - *from a wife.*

6. 'Some professional guidance, involvement, particularly geared towards the needs of our children. I feel that on a personal level my son has coped well with no very obvious 'scars'. This is not the case for all the children, some of whom are still experiencing severe problems. Although over the worst there were times when I did not feel strong enough to cope and lacked real confidence in the ways I did choose to handle my son's problems in coming to terms with his dad's death.' - *from a wife.*

7. 'If the oil companies had acknowledged mothers and fathers as well as wives.' - *from a parent.*

8. 'The opportunity to be involved in a working situation, voluntary or otherwise. For someone to take the trouble to find out what were my special interests or talents and perhaps to find an opportunity for me to be involved in some way. In short to feel useful and needed and have a purpose in life since all purpose had been taken away.' - *from a wife.*

Any other comments

Of the 19 who used the space, seven did so to thank the Social Work Team for their work and a selection of those comments are reproduced here:

1. 'Piper Outreach Team very helpful and supportive to my family.' - *from a son.*

2. 'Without the Team's help and valued friendship the last year would have been very much harder to bear. I, along with many others owe them an awful lot.' - *from a wife.*

3. 'I would just like to take this opportunity to thank all the Piper Outreach Team for all their kindness in our time of need. I don't think we could have come this far without you all especially the home visits. Thank you all once again.' - *from a parent.*

4. 'Thanks for all your Newsletters etc. Words fail me.' - *from a parent.*

The other 12 who used this space had more varied and wide-ranging contributions and their responses are recorded below:

1. 'I know you all did a grand job and I appreciated the Newsletter, but I did find I had to find my own level of "understanding why" and my own objectives now for the future. I not only had my two children to consider, but also my parents-in-law (my husband was an only child) and I did find I was mentally drained at times through 'comforting, advising, appearing strong etc.
   But it paid off - they took strength from me and I now find more support from them because of what I tried to give them during the last year.' - *from a wife.*

2. 'I've found that my doctor and the social worker have been the most helpful and without them we would not have been able to come to terms with this disaster and they have my deepest gratitude.' - *from a parent.*

3. 'There should have been more liaison between members of the same family with regard to the compensation. There have been problems when one lawyer gave full information to me yet my daughter-in-law's lawyer gave her no information. This caused unnecessary heartache and distress. The Social Work Department was of great help and I hope they continue their great work with others in need. I greatly appreciate their help in my time of need.' - *from a parent.*

4. 'In my opinion the Social Work Department did an excellent job; mentally I was able to cope and come to terms with what happened to my husband and sort my future life out, and problems on my own. Some wives and survivors were not able to do this and really benefited a great deal from the help offered to them by the Social Work Department. I knew if I had a problem just to phone and help would be made available to me.' - *from a wife.*

5. 'Piper-Line newsletter most helpful. My family and self looked forward to receiving them and found them most comforting, we felt it helped to share our grief with the other bereaved although never been in contact.' - *from a parent.*

6. 'If I had stayed in Aberdeen I would have had more chance of more contact with other bereaved. It was not a major problem.' - *from a parent.*

7. 'The end of December (1989) is too soon to wind up Piper Outreach - suggest six months after Cullen (Public Inquiry) reports.' - *from a parent.*

8. 'It's a shame that you're expected just to "pull your socks up" and get on with it. Some people heal quicker than others. I'd be a millionaire if I had 10p. for everyone that said "you're young - perhaps get married again one day". I'm sick to death of it. I only know what I feel - and even one year on from the day I lost my husband it still hurts the same - perhaps more. Nothing, no-one can or will replace him. So, the end of December when the social work team

will be going their own ways - the widows (like myself) are still struggling to find theirs. I would love to hold a coffee morning to reach out to others - and have a less formal surrounding in which I could talk and listen. Perhaps someone would take it from there and hold one too.' - *from a wife.*

9. 'It was nice to be able to go and have a chat with the Outreach Team. It was a comfort and very helpful when myself and family were so worried and distressed, it was nice to talk to someone outside the family. We are coping quite well but still feel a great loss.' - *from a parent.*

10. 'I found my family very helpful and have tried to get on with life as best I can.' - *from a parent.*

11. 'We live in a small town and until the disaster did not realise how many caring people there were in this world. Our daughter-in-law and ourselves were visited by every minister in the town, the RC priest and the Salvation Army. Prayers were said for us in most of the churches and we know now that there is power in prayer, as we got strength to face each awful day. We will always be grateful to our friends and neighbours for the help they gave us, and our family have never been so close as they are now.' - *from a parent.*

12. 'Any group such as the Piper Outreach Team is needed after such a disaster for those who feel they need people to talk to as talk is essential. I am very lucky to have an extremely large and supportive family - we are very close so I got, and am still getting, lots of help from them. Even so life is very lonely and I do have depressions but I find I handle these better alone. I find it hard to cry in front of others and to say how I really feel so group meetings were not really for me, but I know others have benefited from them. I liked the Newsletter being sent as this made me feel I knew about what was happening, I just wanted to find out as much as I could about what happened.' - *from a wife.*

Points for discussion

1. What does the questionnaire tell us about the significant sources of help to people bereaved in a major disaster?

2. Consider the answers to Question 7 about other possible services.

3. In the light of the views expressed in the questionnaire, when do you think is the best time to 'wind down' a social work outreach service?

4. Do you think a questionnaire of this kind has value? If so, and you were designing a questionnaire, what questions would you include?

Chapter 7

The survivors: case study

Introduction

This chapter and the following one examine some of the problems confronted by those who survive a major disaster. We will look principally at the sort of things survivors have to overcome following their involvement, on the strains and stresses that manifest themselves in their lives and the lives of their families. We will also look at some of the methods survivors have employed to cope with these problems and their view of the social work help offered to them.

All survivors and their families referred to were involved in the Piper Alpha Disaster of July 1988.

As was stated previously, the term 'survivor' can be taken to include all those 'affected' by a disaster who come through that experience and would thus include rescue staff, police, company personnel, those who were 'nearly there' and so forth. Here, the term is used to cover only those men who were on the Piper Alpha platform when it exploded and who escaped with their lives. They may be best described as the victims who survived, since the effect on their personality of their involvement was subsequently dramatic and fundamental. The phrase most frequently used by their wives in the months following their return was, 'the man who came back is not the one who went away', or a variation on this theme.

One survivor of the Piper Alpha disaster agreed to keep a daily diary of his activities over a one week period in September 1989, some fourteen months after the incident. Extracts of that are reproduced here using social network analysis techniques.

He also agreed to an interview following completion of his diary and that took place in the Piper Outreach Social Work Team office in October 1989.

Problems survivors face.

Survivors of a major disaster such as the Piper Alpha explosion can face problems in a physical, psychological and practical sense. Physical injuries are the first and most obvious impact that may be apparent with survivors. All of the men who escaped from Piper Alpha with their lives were suffering from smoke inhalation damage, most from cuts and bruises, some from broken limbs and a large number from burns injuries.

These ranged from flash burns, to burned hands and feet caused by grasping or crossing metal pipes which were literally melting in the fire, to serious head burns. The two worst burns cases were in this latter group with one man having been caught by a fireball, and the other having had his hardhat melt onto his head. Both received over a year's treatment in the burns unit of the local hospital and effectively had to have the tops of their heads rebuilt.

The 'practical' loss they all suffered was the literal loss of their work-place in the disaster and, for the most of them, an inability to return off-shore to another equivalent installation. A year later, only one of the survivors had returned to work in the North Sea on a regular basis. In other disasters such as earthquakes or floods, survivors have had to come to terms with the loss of their home and possessions. Perhaps most difficult of all, of course, are where some members of a family are killed while others survive. The 'bereaved survivor' was not a feature of the Piper Alpha disaster but would frequently be in a 'natural' disaster or a transport one such as the *Herald of Free Enterprise* capsize.

The area where social workers or counsellors are most likely to come into contact with survivors is in helping to deal with the psychological and emotional aftermath of a disaster. These areas and interventions will be dealt with more fully in chapters 9 and 10. Here, it is important to note that survivors may initially, and not surprisingly, experience feelings of relief and even elation, but these are normally followed by a sense of guilt at having survived when many others did not, at lack of self-worth for not having done more to try and help others survive. This may develop into anger and bitterness directed at the principal company if there is one, as in the case of Piper Alpha, Kings Cross or the *Herald of Free Enterprise*, or at the authorities for not pre-planning sufficiently in the case of a natural disaster.

The syndrome known as Post Traumatic Stress Disorder is frequently experienced by survivors of a major disaster. This, as the name implies, is a collection of stress-related conditions some or all of which might be suffered by them. Among the major items which contribute to this condition are hypervigilence, inability to achieve restful sleep, nightmares, 'flashbacks', pre-occupation with the event, irritability and intolerance, depression, lack of concentration, forgetfulness and hallucinatory experiences.

Clearly a combination of these symptoms over a prolonged period could lead to what would be seen as major personality alterations and thus a cause of stress on those friendships and relationships.

As the following interview, diary and questionnaire results show these problems and stresses did indeed affect in a direct and fundamental way those men who survived the Piper Alpha disaster.

Case Study: Bill Stewart

Bill Stewart is a Glaswegian in his late forties. He had worked on Piper Alpha for many years, employed by a sub-contractor as an electrician on the platform. He has lived with Sheila in a long term relationship following the break up of his first marriage. There are two grown-up children of that marriage but Bill had little close contact with them for some time prior to the disaster.

Bill is a politically active man in the Scottish Trade Union and labour movement and used that commitment and involvement to help him in his recovery process following the disaster. He had been pursuing an Arts course with the Open University and had used his free time on the oil rig and his leave time at home to further his studies.

He suffered minor physical injuries in the explosion and fire and was eventually rescued from the North sea by a Danish stand-by boat.

He has since been actively involved with other survivors and bereaved, and with the Piper Outreach Team and office, being among the most regular users of that facility.

In the fifteen months since the disaster he has managed to continue and broaden his studies. Despite suffering many of the symptoms of Post Traumatic Stress and in particular a serious inability to concentrate for more than short periods, Bill managed to gain acceptance as an Arts undergraduate at a Scottish university. He took up his full time studies there in October 1989.

Interview with Bill Stewart

DT   When you escaped from Piper Alpha, you were picked up by a stand-by boat and eventually flown by helicopter to hospital where you were treated before being discharged. Can you recall your first thoughts and feelings after you left hospital?

BS   They were really rather trivial. I had lost my shoes and I remember apologising to Sheila for that. I was more concerned about her and how she was and hoped I hadn't upset her. Things hadn't really hit me, although before that I had broken down and cried about six times on the boat.
But then, I was really just quite happy to be alive. Not euphoric. I did realise the horrors attached to it all, but did not feel really affected at that time.

DT   Who did you turn to for help at that stage?

BS   I was very fortunate. Sheila's sister Ann came with her to the hospital, she being a psychiatric nurse. I used her for support -

three to four times a day - for months after that. Just talking to her - get things out. She also helped Sheila. Now - she's being funny - when someone asks her what I do for a living, she says "he's a Piper Alpha survivor". She says I've made a career out of it.

Her help initially, and in the longer term, was really quite important. I was told about feelings to expect - guilt, crying, anger and frustration, and the worst of the lot, fits of depression.

Although prepared in that way, it still took me by surprise and I didn't cope as well as I thought. I was disappointed by the lack of medical and psychiatric help apart from physical injuries.

As well as Sheila and her sister, my son (from a former marriage) came up from Glasgow. He was tremendously supportive.

DT   Did you know who else had survived? Did you make contact with them?

BS   No. My son went and bought a newspaper to see the number of dead and the list of survivors. He didn't want to let me see it, but Sheila and her sister both told him it was important to let me see it.

I was more concerned about the widows and phoned up those I knew, especially those whose husbands I had seen that night. I think that was part of the guilt feeling, that I survived that night and their husbands didn't.

A couple of weeks after that I phoned Jim Reid (*another survivor: name changed*).

Because I understand the politics of oil companies I knew there wouldn't be too many vocal against what they were saying at Press conferences. The first thing I did was to contact an MP who's a friend of mine. I hadn't given any interviews or spoken to the Press - they had been in touch, but Sheila just said I wasn't available.

The survivors who spoke to the Press were only telling about how they escaped. Only one talked about what led up to the disaster. It was all about the more human aspects of people the Press were interested in - your background, your age, how you got off. I thought they were irrelevant to the disaster.

The first person who spoke up against the companies was myself. The reason people died was they were waiting for heli-
copters as part of the evacuation procedures. I told them about
the gas leaks and verified others' accounts of the same.

DT When you first received a letter from the Social Work Department,
what did you think?

BS To tell you the truth I can't even remember getting it. Was it maybe
about a fortnight later? Like everything else it was put by and
never answered. I got lots of letters at the time from people
saying that they had read I was there and were happy I survived.
Do you know, fifteen months on I still haven't answered
them. I didn't really think about the Social Work one and because I had other help I didn't think it would be any use or
that I had any need for it.

DT You came to the first survivors' group meeting. Why? What did
you get from that? Was it soon enough?

BS I came to try and get survivors to speak up and do something, and
expose the oil company and not sit back and just take it which
I think a lot of them were, and still are.
Also it gave me an insight into how people were not coping. I
was angry at their inactiveness.
I discovered, and it was quite reassuring, that I wasn't a nutter
- that the feelings and anxieties were shared with others but
angry that they weren't doing anything about it.
I was lucky, I've always been active in the Trade Union movement and because of that I believed things would change and I
still believe it.
Was it soon enough? It should have taken place much sooner.
One reason for that is, I don't think people realised how mentally ill they were, because most of us looked physically alright. If you're physically alright people think you're getting
over it, so, in hindsight I think it should have been called
much sooner. Where were the psychiatrists and psychologists -
they should have been waiting in the hospital when the victims came in who were survivors of the Piper Alpha disaster?
People were naive enough to believe the company would look
after us - that upset me. Only a couple of the divers picked
this up. By this time some of the newspapers had done a job
on us and people were very wary of the press.

DT   Since that time you have been quite closely involved with the Piper Outreach Team. Has this been of use to you or has it hindered you from moving on, by creating a focus for something you'd rather have put behind you?

BS   I think that the relaxed atmosphere and friendliness of the team have made it easy for me to come in and talk to you. It has helped in a lot of ways - I can talk to survivors and bereaved because of the team.

It's terribly important a unit like this was set up and I think we've been very, very lucky with Grampian Region setting it up. The group meetings help you understand your own feelings and realise the other victims are the same.

You can also come along to the Outreach office and speak about the Piper Alpha disaster and you don't see the eyes glazing over, like someone saying 'Oh Christ - fifteen months on - it's time to put it behind you'.

You can come here quite confidently. I think the whole concept of the place is important and I think it is closing too early. To be able to talk and not feel in a medical atmosphere - you come here as equals.

As for dependency or holding me back - no, that upsets me. What about the lads down south - we have to keep sending them newspaper cuttings about what's going on. They say we're lucky - we can come here for comfort, for help, for information, just to talk.

You can be taken away physically from things but not mentally. That's why people from down south phone up all the time and ask what's happening.

A disaster on the scale of the Piper Alpha has been the biggest event of your life so, after fifteen months, the thing is still with you.

Survivors outside Aberdeen have told me that they cannot talk about it because others don't understand and meet them with glib phrases. They can't stand it.

It's definitely not dependency. I choose to come here. You don't tell me. It would be very easy for me not to come here. I make that decision.

DT   You have been heavily involved with other survivors and the bereaved, both individually and in groups. Others have not. Was that the right choice for you?

BS   Yes. I have never felt it was not the right choice. For me it was not
              even a decision I had to think about. It was important I did
              come to meetings not only to help myself but to try and help
              others. I think the involvement helps you think you've got a
              meaning - you're not hopeless and helpless.

DT   What has been the hardest thing to deal with since the disaster?
              How did you manage to cope with it?

BS   I don't think I did manage very well. The obsession with the thing.
              You expect the immediate family to have the same feelings
              and you are not very sympathetic if you see that they don't un-
              derstand. It took a long time to realise that there is life after
              the Piper Alpha and that you have to look at others' needs.
              It's affected all my family - do you start trying to gather your
              life together again to get rid of the obsession - to 'get back to
              normal'?
              Do you start listening to the rest of the news and not just the
              Piper Alpha news. I turn the channel over from one to another
              when the Piper news is finished to see if there is something
              about it on the other one.
              The obsession is a driving force but you've got to realise it's
              unfair - you've got to start caring for others in your life be-
              cause that obsession can destroy relationships, because it leads
              you into emotional blackmail - you just say 'you don't under-
              stand'. Really it's just frustration.
              I really haven't managed to cope with it very well yet. I can
              tell by my concentration level. I can only think about other
              things for short periods and then I drift back to the Piper
              Alpha.

DT   Which things or people have been the most help to you since those
              early days?

BS   Apart from Sheila and her sister, obviously the Piper Outreach
              team. This broadened to help from seeing a psychiatrist and a
              psychologist and a few understanding friends.

DT   Where do you see yourself a year from now?

BS   As I'm changing occupations in mid-life, hopefully I will have
              survived the academic rigours of university.
              I hope I'll be a second year student, because when I enrolled it
              struck me that I have four years tied up and I've never had
              that before. In fact I've never planned one year ahead at any
              time.

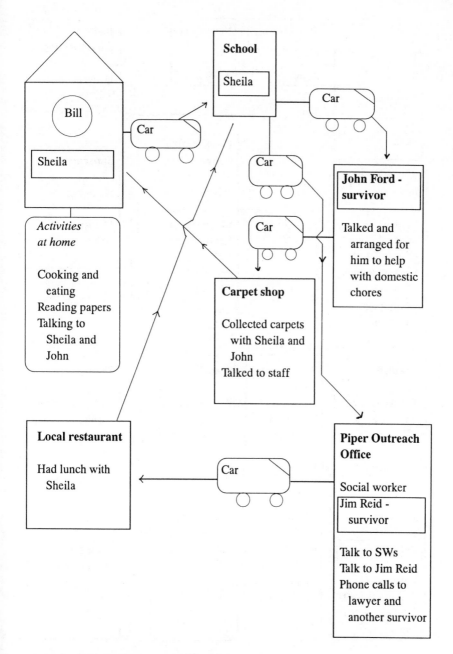

Figure 5 - Diary of Bill Stewart for one day

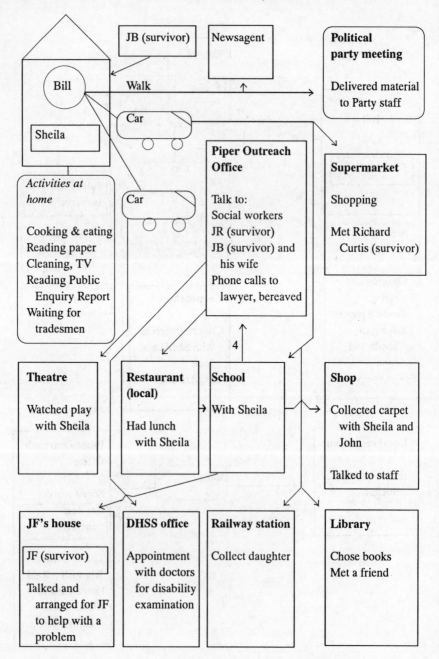

Figure 6 - One week in Bill Stewart's life 14 months after the disaster

I don't think the Piper Alpha will ever leave me. I might be able to cope better and I might have a better understanding of it.

Diary of Bill Stewart

This diary of daily activities was kept by Bill over a week in September 1989 and is reproduced here in diagrammatic form using social network analysis.

Figure 5 shows a day of activities and Figure 6 a week. Bill did not return to paid employment after the Piper Alpha disaster but used his time to study and successfully to gain admission to full-time higher education. Thus there is no work centre represented in these diagrams.

Sheila, with whom Bill lives, is a schoolteacher and as she does not drive, Bill often begins the day by driving her to school. He has continued driving since the disaster but admits to having a number of minor accidents since July '88 largely arising, he maintains, to a certain recklessness he now feels when driving combined with a lack of concentration evident in this as in other parts of his life.

Figures 5 and 6 show clearly that even without regular employment Bill managed to have a busy and active life. His visits to the Piper Outreach office would last from about thirty minutes to several hours. In the course of a single week he records no less than four visits to the office, so he made use of the facilities every day except one in the week recorded.

As Figure 6 shows, it was usually his first call of the day after taking Sheila to school. Although not shown in these diagrams Bill would often drop in on several occasions in one day. The reasons would vary from just to have a coffee and a chat, to meet up with other survivors, to phoning his lawyer, to seeking advice from social workers.

Also, of note, are the number of occasions in a single week that Bill had contact with other survivors of the Piper Alpha disaster. These meetings were not for any specific purpose, nor were they the group meetings organised by the social workers. They were largely informal, or in the nature of friends meeting with each other on a casual basis. As Figure 8 shows, this happened on four separate occasions in one week.

Points for discussion

1. Consider the ways in which Bill Stewart coped with the problems of being a survivor of a major disaster. What were the strengths and weaknesses of his approach?

2. Would regular meetings of survivors in a group forum be likely to benefit them in their recovery, or to hinder them from moving on, by encouraging them to dwell on the disaster?

3. Consider the use Bill Stewart makes of the Social Work Team and comment on how that fits into his pattern of living as shown in Figures 5 and 6.

Chapter 8

Questionnaires to survivors and their partners

A questionnaire was sent to all twenty-one survivors who live in the Grampian area, covered by the Piper Outreach team. One was returned marked 'gone away', and of the other 20 only seven were completed and returned. While this was a rather disappointing return, it could partly be accounted for in that two of the most frequently observed problems among survivors are extreme difficulty in concentrating for anything other than short periods, and also difficulty in confronting or recalling in an overt fashion things which bring memories of the event back. It is noticeable, in this respect, how many survivors of Piper Alpha, and other disasters, break down emotionally when asked to recall events of the disaster at Public Inquiries, often many months later.

Although a small sample, the results are reproduced in tabulated form here and the respondents comments are recorded.

A separate questionnaire was sent out to 46 of the partners of men who survived the Piper Alpha disaster. In the case of Piper Alpha all the partners were female, either wives or girlfriends, and the strains placed upon them and their relationships by being the partner of a survivor was recognised by the social workers early on. Of the 46 sent out, 24 were returned and the answers to the questions posed are tabulated here.

The returns provide an interesting picture of how a group of survivors viewed the social work help offered to them and of how they were coping at the time of completing the questionnaire in September 1989, some 14 months after their involvement in the disaster. When taken together with the much larger response from survivors' partners, a fuller picture begins to emerge of, in particular, the psychological difficulties that confront survivors of a major disaster and their partners and families.

The questionnaires were anonymous but two survivors chose to sign their returns. They were sent with a covering letter explaining their purpose and the use to which returns would be put.

Questionnaire results

1. Have you returned to work offshore or tried to since July 1988?

Yes	No
1	6

2. If not, have you taken up other paid employment?

Yes	No
2	4

(one since ceased)

The one who has continued is working for the same company, but in an on-shore capacity.

Several survivors have tried to return off-shore but had to come home after a day or two.

3. Have you had regular contact with other survivors?

Yes	No
7	-

4. Have you attended any of the survivors group meetings organised by the social workers of the Piper Outreach Team?

Yes	No
7	-

5. If so have you found them
    a) Very useful
    b) Quite useful
    c) Not useful

Very useful	Quite useful	Not useful
6	1	-

6. Have you seen any of the following since July 6th?

    a) GP (other than for minor ailments)
       How often, approx.?

b) Psychiatrist/psychologist
   How often, approx.?

c) Social worker
   How often, approx.?

	0-5 times	*5-10 times*	*10-15 times*
GP	2	1	4
Psychiatrist/ Psychologist	5	1	1
Social Worker	1	3	-

The other three respondents had weekly or more frequent contact with the Piper Outreach Team.

Three of the respondents chose to make comments. One added that he was still seeing a bone specialist at the local hospital. The two other comments are recorded below.

1) 'It is reassuring to be able to speak to someone, without boring them about the Piper.'

2) 'I personally felt that once my feelings (eg personality change and other PTSD symptoms) were explained as 'natural' then I had no further need for counselling. The symptoms still persist, but what can anyone but myself do about it?'

7. Do you feel you were offered enough in the way of help after the Piper?

Yes	*No*	*Other*
5	1	1

(2 with qualifications)

Of the two who answered 'yes' but qualified their response one added 'most of the time' and the other said 'from the Outreach Team and certain psychiatric outlets - yes. From the people who should have helped - the oil company - no'.

The 'other' category survivor commented 'I think so but hard to understand what sort of help is needed'.

8. Do you still suffer from

a) Sleeplessness	4
b) Anxiety/Panic Attacks	5
c) Flashbacks	6

d) Depression   4

e) Feelings of hopelessness/
   pointlessness   2

f) Other symptoms
   - please specify

Among 'other symptoms' listed were lethargy, lack of concentration, forgetful-ness, nervous speech pattern, ill temper, no sexual drive, cannot suffer fools gladly, the world is against me, severe guilt and 'try to punish myself'. One survivor chose to record no answers to this question or to record any comments.

9. What would you hope to be doing in terms of employment and personal circumstances one year from now?

Two of the six recorded no answer and two wrote 'do not know'. The other three comments are recorded below.

1) 'Would hope to be in a better job or working for a different company. Hopefully my wife and I will be in a different house in one year's time.'

2) 'Would hope to be still employed but not necessarily offshore. Personal circumstances will hopefully be improved.'

3) 'A nice steady job with no hassle from superiors. I don't think I could take kindly to orders as my estimation of supervisors took a nose dive on 6th. July 1988.'

10. Is there any particular thing you would have found useful, but were not offered, after Piper?

Three respondents recorded no answer, two answered 'no', one wrote 'would have loved a holiday!!', and one commented 'Immunity from the press'.

11. Any other comments?

Two of the respondents recorded no answer and one wrote 'Thanks for all the help'. The other four made fuller comments and they are recorded below.

1) 'I think the Piper Outreach Team has been a great help to all the survivors. To be able to speak or listen to people who have been through the same thing and who understand what you are saying.'

2) 'The setting up of Outreach was sheer genius. The people staffing Outreach deserve an award. My wife is probably more grateful for your time and understanding than myself.'

3) 'One of the reasons I have not bothered about a job is I don't feel I could give a hundred per cent of my concentration or work commitment to an employer. I start things and then quickly lose interest and as already stated I would react badly to anyone trying to tell me what to do.'

4) 'I think it is far too early to close down Piper Outreach, (after eighteen months), as speaking for myself when I need them I know they are there to help me. There are going to be a lot of people very distressed when there is no one there anymore.'

Partners of survivors

Partners of those who survive a major disaster are liable to be fundamentally affected as a direct result of the incident. They will be expected to live with, and cope with, the victim who survived and whose personality and character may well have undergone transformation. The sleeplessness, irritability, depression, obsession, guilt and other characteristics of the survivor will not only have to be come to terms with by the partner, but their own difficulties in this respect are less likely to be acknowledged by their partner or others than are those of the bereaved or survivors.

Some of the partners of the men who survived the Piper Alpha disaster found they were experiencing extreme difficulties in dealing with their genuine relief and gratitude at having had their husbands or boyfriends return home, while at the same time finding it hard to cope with someone who they felt 'was not the man who went away', and who was now often short tempered, to the point sometimes of violence, obsessed with the disaster and unappreciative of their efforts to understand. The view of others that they were the 'lucky ones', and the exhortations that they must now help their husbands or boyfriends through the post disaster period, did nothing to acknowledge their own needs and difficulties.

The most common way the partners tried to deal with these confused and conflicting emotions and demands was to internalise them and thus suppress the problem. When this, predictably, failed to work, the stresses and strains emerged and many of the relationships were severely tested in the year following the Piper Alpha disaster.

It should be borne in mind that relationships here were not perfectly harmonious prior to the disaster, but were subject to the usual problems and stresses associated with any normal relationship. One additional factor to bear in mind in relation to the Piper Alpha disaster is the work pattern prevalent in the oil industry.

Men who work in the off-shore industry most commonly work a two week on and two week off system. For those for whom this has been an established work pattern over many years, their way of life, as it affects their relationship with their partners, has also been one of being home for two weeks and then absent for the following two.

This pattern of broken or intermittent relationships is in itself often a cause of stress or friction between partners but its sudden disappearance, following the disaster, with the men being constantly at home was in itself a source of problems. Even without the additional stresses caused by Post Traumatic disorders the sudden, unexpected disruption of established relationship patterns could be a cause of difficulty. Together they proved too much for some of the relationships to withstand.

The social workers of the Piper Outreach team organised some group meetings for the partners of survivors living in their area, but in an attempt both to acknowledge the problems partners had, and to try and gauge the nature and extent of the difficulties, they compiled a questionnaire which went, with a covering letter explaining its purpose, to all the partners of the men who survived the Piper Alpha explosion.

Of the 63 men who did survive the disaster, 46 were living with a partner. In July 1989, some twelve months after their partners had survived, these 46 were sent the questionnaire. Twenty-four returned completed questionnaires and the results are tabulated here. Once again a general section for 'other comments' was included and a selection of the responses provided in this section is listed at the end of the tables.

Questionnaire for partners of survivors

1. How long have you been living with your partner?

less than 5 years	5-10 years	more than 10 years
4	5	15

2. How long had he worked off-shore prior to July 1988?

less than 5 years	5-10 years	more than 10 years
3	8	13

3. Did he work a regular shift pattern eg 2 weeks on, 2 weeks off?

Yes	No
21	3

4. Prior to July 1988 did he talk to you about his work?

a little	sometimes	frequently
2	9	12

One answered 'no' to this question.

5. Did he suffer any physical injuries?

yes	no
12	12

6. Does he suffer any emotional distress?

yes	no
24	-

7. Have you noticed any behaviour changes in your partner since the disaster?

yes	no
24	-

8. Did you talk together about how he managed to get off the platform?

  a) If so did he describe his feelings, which may have included fear, panic, guilt?

  b) Did this help you understand why his behaviour might have changed?

yes	no
22	2

Of those who answered 'yes' only one said that the discussions did not incorporate a description of her partner's feelings. She was the only one who expressed the view that the discussions had not helped her understand his changed behaviour.

9. Has you partner been drinking more than usual?

yes	no
14	10

10. Do you argue with each other more than usual?

yes	no
18	6

11. Have you thought about separating?

yes	no
11	13

12. Has the experience of the disaster brought you closer together?

yes	no
12	7

One partner recorded no response and four stated 'yes' and 'no'.

13. Have you had any medical or professional help to support you? (eg GP, psychiatrist. psychologist, social worker, other?)

yes	no
15	8

One made no response.

a) Was this useful?

yes	no
12	3

14. Do you feel that there should be more professional and public awareness for what you have had to go through?

yes	no
22	1

One made no response.

15. Do you think your partner realises the amount of stress placed upon you?

yes	no
11	12

One made no response.

16. Please make any other comments.

Fourteen of the respondents made no entry in this section. Of the ten who did, some used it to express their thanks to the Piper Outreach Team, and others to qualify some of their previous responses. Others used the opportunity to express their feelings and concerns and a selection of their comments are reproduced here.

1. 'People say that time is a great healer and that people forget, but so far I have found this to be less than true. Our lives have changed drastically and I find

it very difficult at times to cope with the unexpected change of moods and long silences.'

2. 'I do at times feel very trapped, he never suggests going anywhere now, preferring to stay at home, so I end up going out alone or with a friend.

   He never laughs anymore, it takes a lot to make him join in socially. The strain is terrible at times, I feel I'm going to explode, that sort of stress is not good for you, but I know he's not well mentally so I bottle it in.

   I wish it was all over, that Piper Alpha never existed, because it's ruining our life. He'll never be the same person and that makes me so angry. My freedom, independence, security, love, support and happiness all disappeared with Piper Alpha. I hope it all comes back soon! Just now I settle for the four walls of the house, the occasional conversation, sarcastic or otherwise, and some happiness gleaned from friends and the children.'

3. 'I feel my life has been changed by the disaster and this sometimes frightens me. I am lucky he survived this and it makes me feel like going on. He has changed in lots of ways, but that is to be expected.'

4. 'Since the disaster my husband is unable to concentrate on anything for too long. Also he has lost interest in doing things e.g. hobbies etc. and tends to want to sit for periods doing nothing in particular. Also he drinks and smokes in excess compared to before the disaster, and is very easily upset and can become bad tempered.'

5. 'We had a wonderful relationship prior to July 6th 1988. Since the accident he is a completely different person, almost the opposite in all ways to what he was before the disaster, and there are times when I honestly dislike him as the person he has become. I only hope that as time passes he may change back to the man I married. I do not think I would like to spend the rest of my life with him as he is now.'

6. 'I do feel the strain when I have to be the strong and supportive one, and when it is the other way round I am told I am miserable and a 'pain' to live with. Because he has been through the experience of the disaster and I haven't I am quite often told "you will never understand". It is difficult at times but at least I am lucky to have him with me, alive and well.'

7. 'I feel I could write a whole book on this subject. I am so glad that you are trying to gather information which may help others in the future.

   The sheer stress of having to cope with a partner whose needs are *so* different and also the stress of always having to think *for* the partner and make sure that any situations are not potentially stressful for the survivor is sometimes overwhelming.

   My husband's moods vary from child-like dependence to absolute defiance and can change in a second with no warning.

I had one visit with my GP because I got to the stage where I could not cope with it any longer and was constantly tired and in tears. I felt guilty about having to ask for help because we are made to feel that we *should* cope - after all we are "OK". The GP was sympathetic and kind but it did not help me because I was still *in* the same situation when I went home. I do not understand why my husband feels like he does and I have supported him throughout the year, going practically everywhere with him and making all arrangements and decisions.

However, I feel that no-one (except yourselves and others in my position) realise the strain and loss of independence and identity.'

8. 'At the beginning of August 1988, no-one considered how wives were feeling. No-one realised what we were going through. We had to keep everything going, house, kids and supporting our husbands.

Everyone asks "how's your husband", not one person ever asked how I was feeling. As months went on, things just kept getting worse, until one day a social worker came to our door, and asked if he could help in anyway. I felt quite funny at first as there is a stigma about social workers, but I got to know him and started to say how I was feeling and he has helped an awful lot even now a year past.

People should be made aware that it's not just the bereaved and survivors that need help; survivors' wives are under a great deal of pressure trying to keep things together; you have to bite your lip sometimes just to keep things going. Please remember the children as they have been affected too - they don't understand what's happening to their father - why he shouts at mummy, and why he shouts at them or tells them to get away. My little one asked if that's what mummies and daddies do. What are you supposed to say to that?'

The answers to the questionnaire are revealing and support other findings in that while only half the survived involved were physically injured, every one was regarded as emotionally distressed by their partners. Every one is regarded as having undergone behavioural changes since the disaster. More than half had noticeably increased their use of alcohol and the vast majority found they now argued much more frequently with their partners than prior to the disaster.

Concerning the conflicting and opposite feelings that sometimes are held simultaneously, half the respondents said they had thought of separating and half said it made them feel closer to their partner. Significant numbers answered yes to both these questions revealing the emotional swings their experience had subjected them to. More than half had sought professional help and almost all felt there should have been more public awareness of their plight and problems.

The comments recorded in answer to the final question stand as a powerful set of statements, attesting to the very real problems that the partners of survivors of a disaster may face.

Points for discussion

1. What does the *Survivors' Questionnaire* tell us about the things survivors experience in a post disaster situation, and how they attempt to cope with them?
2. What does the *Survivors' Partners' Questionnaire* reveal about the problems that group can anticipate in the aftermath of a major disaster?
3. Suggest some ways in which the problems of survivors partners could be acknowledged, and what help could usefully be offered to them by social workers or others.

Chapter 9

Counselling the bereaved

'Tell them, that, to ease them of their griefs,
Their fears of hostile strokes, their aches, losses,
Their pangs of love, with other incident throes
That nature's fragile vessel doth sustain them
In life's uncertain voyage
I will some kindness do them.'

Timon of Athens

Introduction

Following a disaster, social workers can have a valuable role to play in counselling both the bereaved and survivors. 'Counselling' here is taken to mean a focused intervention in peoples' lives designed to help them come to terms with a crisis in their lives and to readjust from it.

This chapter looks at the general way in which social workers can help with those bereaved after a disaster. It will look briefly at the grieving process and at some of the specific problems which may arise in the circumstances of a disaster.

Bereavement

The basic principle to be borne in mind is that each person's bereavement is the worst for them. The fact that, in a disaster situation, their loved one may have died along with a great many others will be, at least initially, irrelevant. It is their own loss and the disruption of their personal world that will be of concern. This was illustrated following the Piper Alpha disaster when one widow, angry at the press categorisation, declared emphatically to the social worker, 'I am *not* a Piper Alpha widow, I am Jim's widow'.

Bereavement is fundamentally a personal experience. No matter the circumstances, it is not a corporate one. Those bereaved in a disaster may well, at a later stage, come to draw strength and comfort from others bereaved in the same circumstances, but initially it is their own loss and pain that will occupy them exclusively.

Whatever the circumstances of the death the person bereaved will undergo a grief reaction categorised by Rapaport as consisting of three broad stages.

'A normal course of grief reaction begins when the bereaved

1) Starts to emancipate himself from the bondage to the deceased.

2) Makes a readjustment in the environment in which the deceased is missing.

3) Forms new relationships or patterns of interaction that bring rewards and satisfactions.'[1]

It is important for the social worker to bear this broad framework in mind, in working with a bereaved person. While general, it nonetheless provides a frame of reference against which to test the progress or otherwise of the bereaved.

When someone is bereaved in sudden unexpected circumstances, such as in a disaster, it is quite normal for there to be an initial stage of acute distress and that may coincide with the time at which the social worker first becomes involved. As with the 'grief reaction' model it is important to understand this, as without this knowledge it becomes virtually impossible to offer any meaningful help. Some research carried out by Lindemann, partly with bereaved disaster victims, deals in detail with this stage.

'The picture shown by persons in acute grief is remarkably uniform. Common to all is the following syndrome: sensations of somatic distress occurring in waves lasting from twenty minutes to an hour at a time, a feeling of tightness in the throat, choking with shortness of breath, need for sighing, an empty feeling in the abdomen, lack of muscular power, and an intense subjective distress described as tension or mental pain. The patient soon learns that these waves of discomfort can be precipitated by visits, by mentioning the deceased and by receiving sympathy. There is a tendency to avoid the syndrome at any cost - to refuse visits lest they should precipitate the reaction, and to keep deliberately from thought all references to the deceased.'

The striking features are:

· The marked tendency to sighing respiration; this respiratory disturbance was most conspicuous when the patient was made to discuss his grief.

· The complaint about lack of strength and exhaustion, which is universal and is described as follows: 'It is almost impossible to climb up a stairway.' 'Everything I lift seems so heavy.' 'The slightest effort makes me feel exhausted.' 'I can't walk to the corner without feeling exhausted.'

· Digestive symptoms, described as follows: 'The food tastes like sand.' 'I have no appetite at all.' 'I stuff the food down because I have to eat.' 'My saliva won't flow.' 'My abdomen feels hollow.' 'Everything seems slowed up in my sto- mach.'[2]

Most of these physical symptoms were indeed reported by those bereaved in the Piper Alpha disaster, and were accompanied initially by feelings of stunned disbelief, followed by anger, guilt and eventually acceptance.

A sudden tragic death is difficult to assimilate for the bereaved partner or parent. Following a disaster, people's understandable hope that their loved one has somehow avoided the tragedy can easily slide into fantasy.

After all the survivors of the Piper Alpha oil rig had been accounted for, some of the bereaved told social workers that they believed their husband was safe and had been picked up by foreign boats, where no one spoke English and that he would phone from some foreign port in the near future. Others insisted that he had not gone to the oil rig, and was unaware of the disaster but would contact them as soon as he heard of it to stop them worrying.

These fantasies, which in most cases did not last long, were made credible to the bereaved because most of the bodies of the men who died were not recovered until many months later.

Generally, the disbelief gave way to anger and bitterness principally directed at the oil companies concerned, but also towards the police, the press and in some cases the social workers. In part this was displaced anger, with the deceased person being the true target, but that was too painful to confront. When someone dies suddenly and unexpectedly, the bereaved often has a sense of being deserted sometimes articulated as 'How could he leave me like this', or 'I just can't cope alone'. The anger and bitterness this leads to has to be directed in some direction, even if inappropriate or undeserved.

There may also be a preoccupation on the part of the bereaved with feelings of guilt. These stem principally from two sources. The first is guilt at things left unresolved, left unfinished. Minor arguments, rows and harsh words may be normal and trivial in most relationships, but when they become unexpectedly the last words, with death removing the opportunity to apologise or make up, then guilt and self remorse can be the result. This is often the reason why grief can be intense even where the relationship was not a particularly close one before death. Guilt and regret are powerful emotions.

Some of those bereaved by the Piper Alpha disaster were separated or estranged from the deceased, but their grief was nonetheless real or powerful for that.

The other main source of guilt felt by those bereaved stems from self reproach. Some of those whose loved ones were lost on the Piper Alpha were still blaming themselves months after the event. 'He didn't want to go that trip, but I made him', 'He was worried about something, but I just wouldn't listen', were two of the variants on this theme.

Role of the social worker with the bereaved

In seeking to work with the bereaved following a disaster, a social worker's role can be looked at under four headings. These are:

1) Being there.

2) Advisor.

3) Information acquirer.

4) Identifying options.

1) Being there

In the early days of a bereavement, just being there is more important than doing anything specific. Being reliable and constant and having time just to be with the bereaved are qualities that are highly regarded. Immediately following a bereavement, people may be almost overwhelmed with the concern of others such as friends, neighbours and above all family. After a bereavement suffered in the course of a disaster one can add the police, company representatives (where there is one involved) and the press to that list. Letters and sympathy cards pour in and the telephone never seems to stop ringing.

All this attention, sympathy, concern and care may help comfort someone bereaved. They may confuse and disorientate them further or they may even be largely unhelpful and intrusive. One thing is certain, and that is they will by and large quickly disappear.

Some family and some very close friends may remain constant in their support but very few others will. Partly this is due to people having their own lives to live, their own concerns and worries to demand their attention and their own families to look after. More powerfully, people find death far too difficult to contemplate. Death is a central taboo in our culture which is seen as best avoided rather than confronted.

In the circumstances of a disaster where the body of the deceased may not have been recovered, as in the Piper Alpha disaster, or may be unrecognisable, as with some victims of the Bradford City Football Club fire, the difficulty people often find in confronting the bereaved is increased.

Common features reported by those bereaved by Piper Alpha included visitors talking about everything except the dead person and, even more commonly, talking about their own experiences of death.

The bereaved often stated their wish to have someone with them, but to sit perhaps in silence for a while. Someone with whom they did not have to feel strong, or whose feelings they did not have to try and protect. In essence, just someone to be there for them and with them.

People's motives in offering comfort to the bereaved often stem from a sense of duty or obligation rather than from genuine concern and their awkwardness often results in the most inappropriate behaviour.

One woman, whose husband died on Piper Alpha, told of a friend who visited and spent several hours talking about how much she wanted to leave her husband and set up home with another man! Another had a neighbour drop in to see her and that ended with the neighbour accusing the widow of avoiding both her and her husband. Many reported being upset by noticing friends cross the street or suddenly enter shops when they saw them. That this reflects the difficulties many have in confronting death rather than a deliberate spurning of a former friend did not help the widows who were left angry and confused by such incidents.

Almost worst of all in this respect were the cliches that people often used to fill awkward spaces. 'Time's a great healer', 'You must be strong for the children', 'In time you will get over it', offer little to someone bereaved in tragic and bewildering circumstances. Most of the men who died on the Piper Alpha platform were relatively young and consequently many of those bereaved were young widows. This factor allowed for the most unhelpful suggestion of all, namely 'You are young and some day you will meet and marry someone else'.

There may well be truth in that statement, as in the other cliches, but it is not what the bereaved want to hear at a time when they have not come to an understanding of what has happened to their loved ones, their family and their life. It may be a statement intended to show that some day their world will again have an order and structure they can be secure in, but it is of little help to them when their current world still seems to be in a state of collapse.

Inappropriate behaviour and unhelpful advice only serve to deepen the anger, confusion, hurt and misery that someone bereaved will be already suffering in the early stages of their grief.

One social worker visiting the bereaved after the Piper Alpha disaster used the occasion of his first visit to define his role as follows:

'If you want to talk about the disaster, that's fine. If you want to talk about other things, that's OK too. If you want to sit quietly and cry a little, I won't interrupt. If there is any practical things need doing, let me know. I'll never say "I know how you feel," because I don't and I won't tell you you'll get over it some day. I'll come for as long as you want me to and I'll stay as long as necessary.'

This statement was really spelling out the limited but nonetheless valuable role he could play. He would help out where he could in terms defined by the bereaved, he would not make things worse by unhelpful statements or actions and above all he would be there after others had stopped calling or visiting for as long as the bereaved felt his presence to be of value.

Sitting quietly with someone who may be wailing in their distress, or sobbing deeply or lashing out in their anger and confusion is no easy task but one that the social worker can fulfil and one which, if he maintains his presence, will pay dividends in that once through that period, the bereaved may come to trust him and use him to help with the rest of the grieving process. This was evident following the Piper Alpha disaster when, as time went on, the bereaved families who had contact with the social workers often said that, apart from the families themselves, the social workers were the only ones who 'really understood'.

2) Advisor

The advisory role that a social worker can assume is based on accrued knowledge and experience. The worker should be acquainted with the physical symptoms often suffered by bereaved people and the kinds of mental pain and stress they will undergo. This knowledge and experience can be useful in normalising the symptoms and feelings to the bereaved. Knowing that these difficulties are common among those bereaved in tragic circumstances does not remove the pain or distress, but it can remove the fear often attached to them. Many bereaved, following Piper Alpha, felt that they were going insane and assurances, based on knowledge, that they were not, did relieve some of the concerns in that area.

In a disaster, body recovery is not always accomplished quickly. The normal grieving process, outlined earlier, is more difficult without a body, and a disturbed pattern is often substituted. Some widows felt that there was something wrong with them because they, although initially sad and distraught, could not really grieve properly without a body, without a service, a funeral or cremation, an opportunity for family and friends to gather in mourning; the accepted rites of passage could not be exercised. For many bereaved by the Piper Alpha disaster, the initial grief lasted for many months before the grieving process could properly begin.

As bodies were recovered many months later, the bereaved began to refer to those whose loved one was positively identified and returned as 'lucky'. This may be perfectly understandable in the circumstances, but little wonder the bereaved began to become very confused when they were applying the language of good fortune to people who had received the remains of their dead husbands or sons after a period of four or five months.

The ability to share with the bereaved person that what they are experiencing or feeling is not abnormal, and help them to understand that the circumstances of the disaster mean that their grieving may not mirror previous experience they have had of death, are valuable roles for the social worker to undertake.

The perceptiveness also to notice when the symptoms or feelings are beyond the normal experience, and to suggest that medical or psychiatric help may be appropriate, is also crucial.

Explaining the reactions of children is another useful function the social worker can undertake. Many of the children whose fathers were lost in the Piper Alpha disaster were very young and they had little understanding of what had happened. Many became very clinging in their attitude to their mother and would become distressed if she were to leave them on their own, even briefly.

All these children really understood was that their father had gone away and left them, and not come back. They were frightened that their mother would do the same. Slightly older children tended to be very protective of their mothers. This involved hiding newspapers with stories of Piper Alpha, turning off the television when news of the disaster appeared. Some teenagers either refused to discuss it at all, or began to offend. Some took to wearing their late fathers' jerseys or jackets. The schoolwork of very many of the children suffered appreciably in the year following the disaster.

Being able to explain the background to the altered behaviour of children often in advance of it occurring allowed the mothers to understand what was happening. Being able to talk to schoolteachers and other members of the family allowed social workers the opportunity to offer meaningful help to some of the children bereaved by the Piper Alpha disaster.

This type of advisory role as it develops in the year or so after a disaster is clearly one where the social worker can be of use to those bereaved.

3) Information acquirer

One constant demand of the bereaved following a disaster is an incessant one for information. After the Piper Alpha disaster this began with a need to know everything about what had happened that night, to a need to have a welter of rumours either confirmed or refuted.

The principal sources of this information are the survivors, the company concerned and the police. Bereaved people, especially in the early stages of their grief, often feel incapable of making painful inquiries and the social worker can undertake some of this on their behalf.

When physically separated from the deceased at the time of the disaster many of the bereaved will have an understandable need to know as much about their loved one's final moments as possible. Above all, they are seeking reassurance that his death was painless, but also being told he was in a certain place with some other people makes it more real for them. It is not perhaps more acceptable but it does confirm that he really was there. This was true of many of the women bereaved by the Piper Alpha disaster.

This information was only available from survivors of that disaster. Many of them found it very difficult to talk to the bereaved, largely because they did not have the information they knew the widows and parents desperately wanted. Many of the bereaved were very reluctant to contact survivors as they knew many were having problems in coping and did not wish to add to their distress. Again, the social workers were able to develop a useful role in acting as a go-between linking the bereaved and survivors either by transmitting information or carefully preparing the ground for personal meetings.

One difficulty with regard to information which gave rise to a good deal of anger following the Piper Alpha disaster was its selective distribution. As things developed in the months following the disaster, the bereaved were not given any regular updating on the cause of the disaster, the body recovery programme, the state of the bodies recovered or other matters which they felt, with some justification, should be first communicated to them. Instead they often read of things first in the press or saw them on TV. What often appeared to them to be a conspiracy to deprive them of first-hand information served to confirm their apparent powerlessness. The social work team decided early on that they would make stringent efforts to share whatever information they received with all the bereaved, and, where appropriate, to consult them on their views.

Information, its gathering and appropriate distribution, is of crucial concern to the survivors and bereaved following a disaster. Although sometimes fraught with difficulties it is an area where, again, social workers can play a useful role.

4) Identifying options

The year or so following the Piper Alpha disaster was one of many hard choices for the bereaved. Social workers found themselves being used as sounding boards or for encouragement to pursue a certain decision. In this area their primary function was to talk through the various alternatives and to offer support to the bereaved in their decision.

VIEWING THE BODY

Perhaps the most harrowing of these concerned the viewing of the body. This dilemma has also been reported in the wake of other disasters, and there are no easy answers, or hard and fast rules to be applied.

The balance between encouraging someone to view an 'unviewable' body and thus remove the otherwise inevitable element of doubt and denial, and encouraging someone to submit themselves to a deeply shocking experience is a difficult one to strike.

Where a body is physically recognisable and when the bereaved's mental and emotional health are reasonably robust, then encouragement to view, with support and preparation before and especially after, is almost always to be encouraged. It removes doubt, it allows the grieving process to continue and it provides an opportunity to say goodbye and begins the process of disengagement. It is still a painful and harrowing experience which almost instinctively others try to protect the bereaved from undergoing.

There is, however, another dimension to this, as Hodgkinson and Stewart indicate:

'It may well be that this protection is more for the benefit of the relative, friend or emergency worker, who fears that the grief expressed may be unbearable.'[3]

In their study of those bereaved in a disaster Singh and Raphael interviewed 36 such bereaved who had not viewed the body of their loved one, having been protected from doing so by well meaning friends, relatives or officials. Of these 36 no less than 22 regretted that decision subsequently and one widow commented that 'No amount of disfigurement could be as bad as my fantasies of how he looked'.[4]

When bodies were recovered after the Piper Alpha disaster, they were returned to the families' undertakers in sealed caskets. The bereaved were actively discouraged from viewing and some families misinterpreted this as meaning they were not allowed to view the body.

There must be a question over the value of viewing a body which is literally unrecognisable either through disfigurement or decomposition. Viewing a badly decomposed body may confer no more acceptance of the reality of a loved one's death than not viewing it. Most of the bodies recovered after the Piper Alpha disaster were only identifiable by means of dental records. To be confronted with an unrecognisable and badly decomposed body could only have confirmed to the bereaved that it was a body they were having returned, but not necessarily *their* body. The possible trauma that such a viewing could entail would be a high price to pay for such uncertainty.

Similarly, after the Bradford Football ground fire 53 bodies were found to be unrecognisable. They were described as follows by one of the social workers involved:

'The badly damaged body may bear no resemblance to humanity, much less the physical appearance of the actual person. The Bradford fire left welded bones in small pools of melted human fat. The relatives did not see these sights.'[5]

The social worker's role in relation to a bereaved person confronted with the dilemma of whether or not to view a body is probably to help to identify the options available and their possible outcomes. The bereaved should be encouraged to talk through the fears and anxieties they have in regard to this matter, and above all should be assured of the support of the social worker before, after and even during the experience, should the bereaved decide to view the body.

At least, in this way, it is the bereaved person who is making the choice and any subsequent regret about the correctness of that decision can be dealt with in the context of having had a real choice. Where the effective choice is removed either by well intentioned discouragement or by official difficulties being placed in the way of viewing, the bereaved may be left not only with a sense of regret but with a feeling of having been cheated.

THE PRESS

Following a disaster the press is a constant factor in the life of the bereaved. The majority of those bereaved in the Piper Alpha disaster were not prepared to talk to or be interviewed by the media. Others decided that, for various reasons, they would talk to the press. Whichever decision they came to, none could escape the effects of the media coverage both in the early days of the disaster and at numerous significant times in the year following.

The social worker can help those in doubt again, by identifying the options and consequences of speaking to the press. After Piper Alpha there were lots of press stories concerning vast insurance payments made to the bereaved, about the huge salaries oil men were reputed to make, about alcohol and drugs on the platforms and so forth. Many of the bereaved were angry and upset at what they saw as these distortions but were faced with giving interviews themselves as the only way they could refute them and put their own views and feelings before the public. Such dilemmas face the bereaved and survivors of all major disasters.

The social workers were able to help the bereaved look at what they wanted to achieve by talking to the press and to pursue that accordingly. More importantly, they were able to advise that some of those who did talk to the press had been met with animosity from some members of their own families who misunderstood the motives behind talking to the media.

In some measure the social workers were able to protect the bereaved by advising the press that they did not wish to give interviews or to be present during them to give support. At the time when the Families Association was establishing itself, the social workers were able to act as a link initially between the group and the press.

THE INQUIRY

Most major disasters will be followed by a Coroners Inquest - a Fatal Accident Inquiry in Scotland - or a Public Inquiry of some description. This is likely to attract a large number of bereaved relatives, at least in the initial stages, seeking to find out what happened and how and why their loved one died.

This is likely to be the first occasion when these relatives will come together - other than for a memorial service - and the social workers can again have a valuable role to fulfil.

After the Piper Alpha disaster, the Public Inquiry under Lord Cullen was established in Aberdeen and commenced its work some six months after the tragedy. As well as examining the events which led up to the disaster, the tragedy itself and ways of ensuring a similar disaster is not repeated, the Inquiry also subsumed the functions of a Fatal Accident Inquiry into the deaths of the 167 men.

Thus, with the relatives on the public benches, the police read out each name, recorded the cause of death, the means of identification and indicated the position of each body recovered on a chart projected by camera onto a large screen. This was preceded by the showing of several graphic videos of the disaster itself and the aftermath.

The tension of the relatives and their grief as their loved one was mentioned and indicated was almost tangible and the social workers' role was to offer immediate comfort to them and in many cases to almost give them 'permission' to leave the hall and then be with them in the small canteen attached to the main hall. All of this went on under the eye of the national press and media and was without doubt one of the most stressful and difficult times for both relatives and the social workers. This anxiety and grief in a public setting are features of bereavement after a disaster not normally encountered in other circumstances.

Many of the relatives indicated that that period felt exactly like the time they were first told of their loved ones' death. The grief and anguish were almost uncontrollable, the anger came flooding back and they were almost bereaved again. Mirroring this, the social workers' role regressed to that which it was in the very early days; principally, being there. The difference was that this time there were large groups of relatives rather than individuals.

The Inquiry also provided the first occasion when the bereaved and the survivors came into contact with each other. Again, social workers found themselves acting as brokers and intermediaries between the two groups, who found it difficult to breach the physically small gap across a canteen unaided.

Another function the social workers had in relation to the Inquiry was in the disseminating of information. Because the victims and the families of the Piper Alpha disaster lived in all parts of the UK and abroad, not all either could, or wanted to travel to Aberdeen to attend the proceedings. Many, did, however want to know what was happening and would phone the social work office almost daily for updates, or to request copies of documents or transcripts.

Many of the relatives who did attend the Inquiry were constantly faced with the dilemma where they wanted to attend and to hear and see everything relating to the death of their husband or son, while at the same time not wanting to go through the pain and anguish that attending brought with it. Talking through these alternatives with the social workers proved valuable for many and some did acknowledge that having the social workers support and presence actually at the Inquiry helped them to undertake this painful task.

In many ways, the social work role with the bereaved at a Public Inquiry is a microcosm of their overall role. It varies from being there to offer comfort and support, to advising on what is happening and on some of the more judicial proceedings, to collecting and distributing information, to helping identify alternatives and supporting the relatives in their decisions.

Points for discussion

1. What differences in approach would be appropriate when first seeing a bereaved disaster victim as opposed to someone bereaved in more normal circumstances?

2. Consider different means of helping someone bereaved in a disaster who refuses to accept their loved one is dead.

3. What particular problems might grieving without a body give rise to? What kinds of help can be offered to someone in this position?

4. What are the main things to bear in mind in counselling children who are bereaved?

5. In this chapter the social worker is categorised as having four broad functions in relation to the bereaved. In what other areas might they offer help?

References

1. Rapaport, Lydia (1962). *The State of Crisis: Some Theoretical Considerations*. University of Chicago Press.
2. Lindemann, Erich (1944). Symptomatology and Management of Acute Grief. *American Journal of Psychology*, Sept.
3. Hodgkinson, P. E., and Stewart, M., (1988). Missing, Presumed Dead. *Disaster Management*, 1.
4. Singh, B., and Raphael, B., (1981). Post Disaster Morbidity of the Bereaved. *Journal of Nervous Mental Disorders*.
5. Hodgkinson, P. E., and Stewart, M., *op. cit.*

Chapter 10

Counselling the survivors

Background

Work with the survivors may be identified in three areas:

- a) Individual work
- b) Public work
- c) Linking-up.

Before being able to do any useful work with those who survive a major disaster, it is important to have some understanding of how such a traumatic event may affect those who survive it.

As mentioned before, all of the men who survived the Piper Alpha disaster suffered physical injuries ranging from smoke inhalation to minor cuts and bruises to major burns injuries.

The psychological and emotional disturbances affecting survivors are the areas where social workers can have a useful role. Not unnaturally, most of the men who survived were initially relieved and grateful to be alive and re-united with their families.

Some held parties or other celebrations, while others talked to the press of their great relief and gave details of their escape. Almost all found that these feelings quickly gave way to guilt and depression. The sadness of losing 167 of their friends and colleagues was compounded by feelings of guilt engendered partially by their own relief and celebration in such circumstances. Guilt is also a feeling reported by survivors of other disasters. Those who emerge with their lives from such an event often feel guilt that they did so while so many others did not.

These symptoms are often the prelude to a condition known as Post-Traumatic Stress Disorders, now identified as likely to affect those involved in a major disaster.

In their work on this condition among international rescue workers, Paton, Andrew and Cox highlight the significant features of this condition as follows:

'The classification of post-traumatic stress disorder is defined in the American Psychiatric Diagnostic System (DSM III). The diagnostic criteria described are as follows:

A. A recognisable stressor that would be expected to evoke significant symptoms of distress in almost all individuals...

B. Re-experiencing the traumatic event either by

1. Recurrent and intrusive recollections of the event; or

2. Recurrent dreams of the event; or

3. Suddenly acting or feeling as if the traumatic event were occurring because of an association with an environmental stimulus...

C. Numbing of responsiveness to, or involvement with, the external world beginning some time after the traumatic event(s) as shown by either-

1. Markedly diminished interest in one or more significant activities; or

2. Feelings of detachment or estrangement from others; or

3. Marked constriction of affective responses...

D. At least two of the following (not present prior to the traumatic event)

1. Hyperalertness or exaggerated startle response;

2. Initial, middle or terminal sleep disturbance;

3. Guilt about surviving when others have not, or about behaviour required to achieve survival;

4. Memory impairment or trouble concentrating;

5. Avoidance of activities that arouse recollection of traumatic event;

6. Intensification of symptoms by exposure to events that symbolise or resemble the traumatic event.[1,]

A more detailed list of how these symptoms are manifested is contained in the three sections of the Stress response Rating Scale compiled by Weiss, Horowitz and Wilner.[2] They are classified under 1) intrusion items; 2) denial/avoidance items; and 3) general items.

Knowing something of the signs and cause of post-traumatic stress disorders is important for the social worker working with survivors of a disaster, as it enables him or her to understand the problems and difficulties a survivor may be facing and also provides a framework of reference which allows him to locate the problems being encountered.

Armed with this information the social worker is then in a position to offer assistance in the three areas previously identified.

1. Individual work

In working with survivors of a major disaster, the social workers' principal task is to help them come to terms with the experience they have undergone. People will do this in different ways and have differing responses to their experience; but some similarities do emerge.

After the Piper Alpha disaster, those who survived found an almost compelling need to talk about the experience. This was often at length and repetitive but was a way in which they tried to reach an understanding of what had happened.

The social workers encouraged them to do this and provided an audience for them. Crucially, they continued to do this long after others had become bored and moved on. This fact was one of the things most commonly mentioned by Piper Alpha survivors - that the social workers and their office remained as an opportunity to talk about the disaster with the security that no-one's eyes would glaze over, no-one would start glancing at their watches.

With Piper Alpha survivors, it was necessary on some occasions almost to give 'macho' oil-men permission to have emotions, feelings of sadness, weakness and grief.

When the symptoms of post-traumatic stress disorder began to manifest themselves, it was important that the social worker was able to identify them as a recognisable and understood condition. This did not remove the problem but it did help alleviate the fear of the symptoms which often led survivors to believe that the events of that night were leading to madness.

Similarly, being able to label and partly explain the syndrome to the survivors' wives, at least allowed them some understanding of what their husbands were going through, and why they were acting in unusual and apparently inexplicable and disturbing ways. It was also an opportunity for the social worker to acknowledge their very real needs and concerns.

Being able to link the survivor to help in the psychiatric services where the disorders are acute is another important function the social worker can undertake.

So, in working with survivors of a disaster, the social workers' tasks may be described as grief counselling, explaining the responses of victims to traumatic events, family counselling and above all continued availability for the survivor and sustained interest in the survivor. In effect, helping the survivor to understand what has happened to him or her, helping to cope with the effects on himself and his family and aiming towards a time when he can move on from the traumatic event. As one social worker put it after the Piper Alpha disaster to a survivor, 'You will always be a survivor of Piper Alpha, but one day you will stop only being a survivor of Piper Alpha'.

Public work

The press

Following any disaster, those who survive are sought out by the press and media anxious for their stories. Like the bereaved, most simply refuse to have anything to do with them while others, in their initial relief or euphoria, happily give interviews. After Piper Alpha, many came to regret this, having made remarks which may have been jocular in the heat of the moment but in the cold light of day looked callous or insensitive. Over the months to come the press continued to seek them out and, as with the bereaved, the social workers were able to discuss the pros and cons of agreeing to or refusing press requests.

As time went on there were occasions when some of the survivors actively wanted to talk to the press to have their individual or collective view put over to the public. This happened on issues such as payments from the Piper Alpha Disaster Fund, insurance payments, compensation settlements and so forth. On these occasions they were able to use the social workers to work through their feelings and anxieties, to rehearse their statements and even to make the necessary arrangements to meet the journalists.

The inquiry

Almost every disaster is followed by an inquest or a Public Inquiry, at which survivors and other witnesses will be called on to give evidence.

This is likely to be a severely traumatic time for survivors and it is again one where the social worker can have a useful role.

The Piper Alpha Inquiry began some six months after the disaster. It took place in a large hall, at an Exhibition Centre and as well as Lord Cullen who conducted the proceedings there were three technical assessors sitting on a raised dais. In front of them were ranks of Advocates (QCs), solicitors and other officials representing a wide variety of interests. Further back were the press and media and then the tiered ranks of seats for the bereaved relatives and other members of the public.

The various lawyers and counsel did not wear their court gowns and wigs, but the procedures were judicial and the atmosphere similar to a courtroom.

In these surroundings the survivors were called on to recall and relate in detail the events of the disaster. For many it proved too difficult and the proceedings were regularly halted as the survivors broke down or simply could not carry on with their evidence.

By and large, the ones who had been in regular contact with social workers and had attended the survivors group meetings coped better with this than did those who up until that time had had little contact or tried to deal with the pain by internalising it and repressing it.

The social workers took on the role of briefing the survivors about the proceedings and formalities and encouraged them, where possible, to visit the Inquiry prior to giving evidence to at least acclimatise themselves. They were also available to be with the survivors before and after they gave evidence and with the court's approval were also allowed to accompany survivors into the witness box. This support role, which is unique, was used by a large number of the Piper Alpha survivors and was one which all later stated was very helpful to them in getting through this harrowing task.

Linking-up

The final important role the Piper Alpha social workers had in relation to the survivors was in linking-up. When carrying out initial visits to the survivors at home they most often wanted to know who else had survived, how badly injured they were and if they could be contacted.

Working on an oil rig is a strange working environment. Although the men were physically close together for the two weeks on the rig, or perhaps because of it, few of them were close friends when on shore. Physically they lived all over the UK and so would separate at the airport and often not see each other until they met again at the airport two weeks later. So, while they knew each other, by and large they didn't know much about each other. This was well illustrated by one survivor who asked the visiting social worker to bring him a list of all the survivors but when that was done, found he could make little use of it since everyone on the oil-rig was known by nick-names. The official survivors' list meant nothing to him.

Linking-up survivors with friends or work mates was a difficult but rewarding task that the social workers undertook. Survivors of Piper Alpha were in a unique position in that way, since it is unlikely that people who happened to book a passage on the ill-fated Herald of Free Enterprise or boarded the tube involved in the Kings Cross disaster would have any prior knowledge of their fellow survivors.

What the social workers were able to do in all these cases was to set up and then facilitate survivors' group meetings which all known survivors could attend. After Piper Alpha, the Grampian social work team set up such a group but it was restricted to those living in the Grampian area. Other groups were established by others in different parts of the country. The group is looked at in more detail in the next chapter.

Linking survivors up in an individual way, where appropriate, or in group settings; helping and supporting them in their public role following a disaster, and offering them and their families help in coming to terms with what they have experienced and with beginning to move on from it, are the main tasks facing social workers with survivors following a disaster.

Points for discussion

1. What advice could be offered to someone who has just survived a disaster as to what he or she may anticipate?

2. The social worker is described as having three areas of concern in relation to survivors. In which other areas may the social worker have a contribution to make?

References

1. Paton, Andrew, Cox (1988). A Preliminary Investigation into Post-traumatic Stress In International Rescue Workers. Research Report No.1. Applied Social Science Unit. Robert Gordons Institute of Technology. Aberdeen. 1988.
2. Weiss, Horowitz and Wilner (1984). Stress, Response Rating Scale. *Journal of Clinical Psychology* 1984.

Chapter 11

Group work

Introduction

It has been seen that following a disaster, social workers may initially offer a telephone helpline and counselling service. This might be followed by a pro-active offer of individual and family based support and counselling. Once that is underway it may be useful to offer group meetings to sections of the disaster affected population. This chapter looks at some of the thinking behind this approach and at some of the groups established following recent disasters.

Background

Groups can be designed to be therapeutic in that their purpose will be ultimately to effect some change in those attending. Alternatively, they can be established with less well defined goals and aims, but may nevertheless have some therapeutic advantage for those attending. Even if the latter model is the favoured one, the groups should have some explicit purpose or they may become just social gatherings to which admittance is achieved by virtue of a connection to the disaster. This type of social association may have some value but, if the purpose of the group is either ill defined or not prescribed in some way, those who choose to attend may have their expectations raised but not fulfilled.

To be purposeful, a group will need to have at least three broad strands. These can be categorised as follows:

1) An opportunity to share experiences and feelings.

2) An instillation of hope.

3) A forum for education about human responses to traumatic incidents.

Those organising and facilitating the groups need to be aware of these three functions and it is, at least in part, their role to see they are achieved.

An opportunity to share feelings and experiences.

Being involved in, or directly affected by a major disaster is something that will only happen to a minority of people. It is a unique experience, and one which those affected often feel they can only truly share with others who have been through the same experience.

Individuals often feel unwilling to burden other family members and friends with their own problems and may find that they can only truly share their feelings with others involved who they believe will understand and not reject them.

The benefits of this type of sharing are attested to by participants following the *Herald of Free Enterprise*, Bradford Football Fire and Piper Alpha disasters. It is also advanced in a more general sense by Yalom in his categorisation of Universality.

'Many patients enter therapy with the disquieting thought that they are unique in their wretchedness, that they alone have certain frightening or unacceptable problems, thoughts, impulses and fantasies... In the therapy group, especially in the early stages, the disconfirmation of a patient's feelings of uniqueness is a powerful source of relief. After hearing other members disclose concerns similar to their own, patients report feeling more in touch with the world and describe the process as a "welcome to the human race" experience. Simply put, the phenomenon finds expression in the cliche, "We're all in the same boat".'[1]

For some groups adversely affected by their involvement in a disaster, the ability to share the experience is recorded as a major coping strategy. In their work on post-traumatic stress disorders among international rescue workers[2] Paton, Andrew and Cox record the most effective coping strategies:

1. Talk to others about event

2. Seek out others dealing with the same thing.

3. Seek increased emotional support from others.

4. Talk through events with workmates.

5. Talk through events with friends.

An instillation of hope

The sharing of a powerful experience may bring a sense of relief and ease concerns about uniqueness, but that needs to be allied to a sense of hope that the crises and their symptoms will come to an end, and that life can again be pleasant and safe.

On a very basic level, if the group setting does not provide the participant with some sense of hope, some positive view of the future, it becomes more likely that the participant will cease to attend and thus miss out on other available elements, such as sharing, progress of others, and the educative content.

Instilling a sense of hope through the group setting can also help offset the initial sense of hopelessness disaster affected victims may feel in other environments. Commenting on this function of the group in relation to those affected by the Mexico City Earthquake disaster in September 1985, Dufka records:

'As clients attempted to reorder their lives as parents, students or workers, they were confronted with a sense of desperation and fear that life would never again be joyful or normal. Twenty year old R described her disappointment in returning to her classes at the university to find them completely irrelevant. Forty year old Y described the emptiness he felt both at home and at work and his fear that it would never dissipate. Amid the destruction, the media coverage, and the constant reminders of the tragedy, it was essential that workers convey hope and assurance that all crises eventually end.'[3]

So, while people involved in a disaster may initially attend a group to share feelings and experiences, and gain relief and reassurance that their experience is not unique, they are likely to continue to attend if they also find hope for the future.

This may take the form of re-assurance from social workers or other group participants, either in general or at particularly critical times, or it may come from the experience of some other group member who is further along the road to recovery than they are themselves, and can thus provide a model or practical example of what can be accomplished.

A forum for education

The social worker can fulfil a useful function with groups in explaining some of the ways in which normal people react to abnormal circumstances.

To explain to people that being bereaved in the sudden tragic circumstances of a disaster may result in them feeling numbed, angry, unable to accept, to see and hear the dead person can bring a sense of relief. To have their symptoms 'normalised' in this fashion is as important as to discover by sharing that their symptoms are not unique to them.

Similarly, with those who survive a disaster, using the experiences and post-disaster reactions of those who survived previous disasters, helps to 'normalise' their symptoms and to remove the fear that these may presage madness. Again, the sharing, in the group setting, of symptoms and having others confirm that they are undergoing them too almost always brings relief and hope.

This was certainly true of the groups established following the Piper Alpha disaster and this, allied to the anticipation of future problems which the social workers were aware may have developed, proved enormously useful to participants.

Again, the experience of post disaster work recorded by Dufka following the Mexico City earthquake mirrors the experience almost exactly.

'Clients commonly expressed concern that their response or the response of their children was abnormal. This concern was particularly prevalent among those who had experienced delayed symptoms. Lack of communication among friends and family members exacerbated this belief. Even if this fear of 'going crazy' as so many clients described it, was not verbalised, the worker explained that symptoms such as anxiety, memory loss, inability to concentrate, intrusive thoughts, dizziness, depression, disturbances in sleeping and eating patterns and startle reactions were normal. This assurance was almost always met with expressions of relief.'[4]

The groups

Following recent disasters, the formation of groups to offer help to specific clusters of those affected has become a feature of the longer term response. Although they sometimes had slightly different titles depending on the nature of the disaster the major groups identified are:

1) Survivors and families
2) Bereaved next of kin
3) Parents
4) Families' Associations

1. Survivors and families

Following the Piper Alpha disaster, the social workers were encouraged to establish groups as a result of their initial visits. The first ones to express this desire were the survivors - those who had been on the Piper Alpha platform and had escaped with their lives.

The first meeting was organised in a local hotel exactly two months after the disaster and invitations were issued to the 21 men who lived in the Grampian area. Nine of these turned up and four others from outwith the area also came. The group continued to meet on a monthly basis, approximately, for the following 17 months and 18 of the 21 Grampian survivors attended at least one of the meetings. As may have been anticipated, the early meetings attracted the largest attendances, with numbers dwindling towards the end. There were sharp increases in attendance to coincide with significant events.

The relating of escape experiences and recollection of events immediately prior to the disaster were features of the very early meetings. Later ones concentrated on the sharing of emotional and physical problems as well as financial ones. Anxieties prior to giving evidence at the Public Inquiry and concern, by some, at meeting the bereaved were recurring features for a time.

As well as providing these therapeutic elements, the survivors' group became a forum for a time which enabled the participants to act in a collective manner when required. There was some concern in the early days of the group that survivors were being unfairly treated in the matter of disbursement of funds from the Piper Alpha Disaster Fund. The survivors used the group to express their feelings and their anger and to fashion a collective response. They began to issue press releases and call press conferences to counter what they saw as their being ignored or their needs misunderstood by others.

They were able to adopt similar collective stances over the year following to such issues as being made redundant, lack of insurance cover, compensation payment offers and so forth. Other survivors, who lived outside the catchment area, were able to communicate with the group via letters or phone calls to be related by the social workers.

The first group offered help following the *Herald of Free Enterprise* sinking were the crew survivors, principally because they were the most easily identified.

The social workers involved following the Kings Cross tube disaster offered group support both to direct survivors and to traumatised London Regional Transport staff.

SURVIVORS' PARTNERS

It would be very easy to overlook the needs of survivors' partners when planning a group response. After Piper Alpha, all the partners were female, ie wives or girlfriends. The social workers first identified their particular problems in the course of visiting the survivors. Subsequently, the issue was raised again at a survivors' group meeting when the men there were discussing how difficult their partners were finding things and acknowledging that they themselves placed great demands on their wives or girlfriends. A significant number of relationships did not withstand these pressures and the couples separated. In some cases there may have been reasons for this which pre-dated the Piper Alpha disaster, but at very least the personality changes that occurred as a result of the disaster were a contributory factor in the breakdowns.

The social workers offered a group meeting to the partners of the Grampian survivors and nine attended the first one and decided to meet monthly thereafter. From this a core of six emerged and they continued to meet for several months to discuss mutual difficulties of living with someone who has survived a disaster.

Other wives and girlfriends from outwith the Grampian region chose to make use of the social workers for help in this area either by phone, or on occasional visits to Aberdeen, but on an individual basis.

The particular types of difficulty this group encountered and their responses to them are best attested to in the results of the previously cited questionnaire to survivors partners (Chapter 6).

COUPLES GROUP

In an attempt to help survivors and their partners share the difficulties each faced with each other, in a neutral setting, the social workers organised an evening meeting for survivors and their partners to attend together. This did not prove a successful format with only two couples making use of the initial meeting and only one returning to a subsequent one.

It may be that the idea was too confronting but a number of couples did continue to use social workers, but on an individual basis, to try to come to an understanding of the difficulties and pressures they were imposing on each other and to work with the social worker towards resolving the problem.

2. Bereaved wives group

Following the Piper Alpha disaster, the social workers set up two groups for the widows of the men who died. One was located in the north of Grampian Region and the other in Aberdeen. Grampian is a large region and while the widows in the northern part did wish to meet with others, it would have taken them several hours to travel to Aberdeen.

The two groups met monthly and allowed those attending an opportunity to share their feelings. They also provided an opportunity for some to form friendships and support each other on a day-to-day basis.

In addition, a local church minister, in association with a volunteer from Cruse, established a weekly meeting for about half a dozen women who lived in the part of Aberdeen where the church was located.

At a later date the social workers organised a more overtly social affair in the form of a coffee morning. This attracted a large response, including many women who had not taken up the opportunity to attend the more formal group meetings. Whether those attending felt that the format was less threatening or whether it was simply a concept they were more familiar with and therefore more comfortable in responding to, is uncertain. What is clear is that it proved an attractive offer to the bereaved and was successfully repeated on a number of occasions.

Again, Piper Alpha was probably unique in modern day disasters in that all those who died were male, and this fact obviously influenced the offers of help directed towards the surviving spouses.

Following the *Herald of Free Enterprise* sinking, group support was offered to bereaved parents of young children, crew survivors and parents of adult children who died. They also had the problem of addressing the needs of the bereaved survivor as well as other survivors and next of kin. The focus for group support following that disaster was much more widely based than it was following the Piper Alpha tragedy.

Following the Kings Cross fire group support was offered, in addition to LRT staff and survivors, to bereaved families, to the injured and to the emergency services.

3. Parents group

As was mentioned before most of the men who died on the Piper Alpha platform were relatively young. All the public concern and the media interest seemed to centre around the plight of the bereaved widows and children. Most of those who died still had one or both parents living and when social workers did make contact with them they were often met with statements along the lines of 'we are the forgotten people in all this'.

A group was formed to allow these parents to meet with each other and to acknowledge their needs and their loss. The first two were well attended, but were amongst the most difficult meetings of all. Having your children pre-decease you is almost unbearable for many people and sharing their grief and misery seemed to offer little to them.

This was also true of some parents who chose not to attend the group but did see a social worker on an individual basis. For many their grief and loss was compounded by their feeling of being the 'forgotten ones' in the disaster, and in a significant number of cases further exacerbated by splits which developed in the family between them and their daughter-in-law. In many cases the parents and bereaved wife of the deceased offered each other a good deal of support and care, but in some cases they became significantly rivalrous.

The reasons for the disputes were many and varied, but the roots of it often lay in the perception of the deceased as 'my son' as opposed to 'her husband'. It was ownership of the memory of the deceased that was at stake.

The loss of an adult son, the upset in the 'natural order' by pre-deceasing the parent, the circumstances of the death, the feeling of being forgotten and the some-times rivalrous behaviour of other family members, left the parents among those most broken by the Piper Alpha disaster.

The group continued for some time with a small core emerging who found it a useful opportunity to share feelings and reminiscences, but its lack of a therapeutic dimension rendered it inappropriate for most parents.

4. Family Associations

Many disasters eventually give rise to Family Associations or Action Groups con-nected to them. This was true of the *Herald of Free Enterprise*, the Manchester air crash, the Kings Cross tube fire, the Lockerbie air disaster, the Piper Alpha tragedy and the Hillsborough Football Ground disaster.

These tend to have fairly political agendas and to have a campaigning element to them. Often they will be seeking 'justice' for those lost, in some cases increased safety measures, in others prosecution of those seen as responsible.

They also provide a way of offering continued support and contact to relatives once the social workers have returned to their original posts. In at least two cases they took over the newsletter title and circulation after social work support ceased.

Social work's principal input to such groups comes in helping them to get established and to organise their early meetings. This was very much the case with the Piper Alpha Families and Survivors Association.

Offering additional information and support in the early days may help them to cohere as a group but involvement in the formulation or pursuit of their objectives would probably be inappropriate and almost certainly unwelcome.

Helping to establish something which can be left in place to offer support to disaster affected victims once other agencies have withdrawn, is the key social work role in relation to this type of association.

Conclusion

Using the group model as one way of offering help and support to people after a disaster can be a very positive development.

Clearly, the types and numbers of such groups will be determined by the nature and scale of the disaster and to some extent by the information about relatives, survivors and others made known to the social workers.

The success or otherwise of such groups, in so far as they are of benefit to the participants, does seem to depend crucially on the group facilitators being aware of, and having a sense of, the purpose of the group.

Organising and publicising the initial meetings of a group provides the opportunity to help. Being able to develop and make use of that opportunity is the task of the social worker.

Points for discussion

1. The Piper Alpha victims were mostly young and all of them were men. How, if at all, would these features affect your group work practice?

2. Illustrate the three functions of groups: (a) experience sharing, (b) hope sustaining and (c) educating.

3. In what circumstances might a group approach be seen to be inappropriate?

References

1. Yalom, Irvin, (1985). *The Theory and Practice of Group Psychotherapy*. Basic Books, New York, 1985.
2. Paton, Andrew, Cox, (1988). *A Preliminary Investigation into Post Traumatic Stress in International Rescue Workers*. RGIT, Aberdeen.
3. Dufka, Corinne, (1988). The Mexico City Earthquake Disaster. *The Journal of Contemporary Social Work*. Family Service America.
4. Dufka, Corinne, *op. cit.*

Chapter 12

The newsletter

Introduction

The use of a newsletter in the aftermath of a disaster is one strategy that social workers have developed since the Valley Parade Football Ground fire in 1985. It has been used after a number of disasters since then, but most notably after the *Herald of Free Enterprise* tragedy, the Kings Cross Tube fire, the Piper Alpha disaster and most recently after the Hillsborough disaster.

The newsletter has a number of specific functions, but has two overall purposes. The first is to provide an effective, relatively simple means of linking a disaster-affected population who may live in many parts of the country and even abroad. The second purpose is described by Michael Stewart in writing about the *City Link Newsletter*, established in the aftermath of the Bradford disaster.

> 'It was to become for a great many the only acceptable place to share a feeling, to divulge a problem, to ask a question. Here at least, the audience would understand. Here there was no stigma. One could rest assured that no one would pry.'[1]

After the *Herald of Free Enterprise* disaster the social workers issued *Herald Link* and produced four editions over the first year. The Newsletter was eventually taken over by the Herald Families Association when the social work team was withdrawn. The same pattern was repeated after the Kings Cross Tube disaster when again four editions of the Newsletter were produced under the auspices of the social workers and was subsequently taken over by the Families Action Group.

The *Piper-Line Newsletter* was produced by the Piper Outreach Team of Grampian Regional Council following the Piper Alpha disaster and ran to eight editions in the eighteen months of that team's existence. Following their disbandment the Piper Alpha Families and Survivors Association took over the title.

Functions

1. Information

Carrying information of particular relevance to the Newsletter's audience is an obvious and primary function. This function was highlighted as the principal reason initially behind the production which was used as part of the recovery activities after the Australia Post Building shootings in 1987.

'Regular production of a Newsletter for staff and families, first containing news of injured colleagues, the bereaved and later poetry, prose, compensation and fund-raising details.'[2]

So while the Newsletter is a good means of linking a widely dispersed population after a disaster like Piper Alpha or the *Herald of Free Enterprise*, its value can also be seen where the affected population are physically close together.

The *Piper-Line Newsletter* regularly carried information about the arrangements for, and subsequent proceedings at, the Public Inquiry. Additionally, articles appeared on arrangements for Memorial services, proposals for a Families Association, issues concerned with compensation, and the availability and location of group meetings.

The information articles were very much appreciated by those people who lived outside the North East of Scotland, as they often commented that apart from major events - such as the opening of the Public Inquiry, and the raising of the accommodation module from the sea-bed - the national press quickly lost interest. This tended to increase their sense of isolation and many commented that Piper-Line was the only means they had of keeping in touch with developments.

2. Education

The Newsletter can also perform a valuable role in alerting people to the facts about issues such as stress, grieving and loss. Passing this on to a disaster affected population can be an important part of normalising the feelings that people may be experiencing. As stated previously, this may not relieve the pain and suffering but may well allay some of the fears associated with them. Additionally, sharing information about how people coped in the aftermath of previous disasters can help by reinforcing the notion that others have gone through similar crises, how they felt and coped, and, crucially, survived them. The instillation of a sense of hope and the knowledge that the worst of the feelings will end can be an enormously useful function for a Newsletter to undertake.

To this end the second edition of the *Piper-Line Newsletter* produced for those affected by the Piper Alpha disaster, carried an article entitled 'After Stress' which listed some of the symptoms which people might expect to experience after a traumatic incident. It also carried a letter from some of those who had survived the *Herald of Free Enterprise* disaster. That letter included the following paragraph:

'Things will never be "the same" again as we have changed due to our experience, but it is not all negative as gentle persons have become more assertive and aggressive people have become gentler. It's different but it's OK as we get to know our (new) selves better. Don't be frightened to ask for help; it's too difficult to do it alone.'[3]

This general message was reinforced by an article written by a psychologist in the anniversary issue of the same publication. In his article he stated:

'Unfortunately, society seems to offer only a limited time scale within which those who have been affected are expected to "get back to normal". Not only is the time scale an unrealistic one but the very idea that people whose lives have been disrupted by the disaster could ever get back to "normal" is naive and unhelpful. Their lives will always be different; what they have to do is to learn to live with the consequences of the disaster and come to terms with what has happened ... One of my concerns is that the victims may feel overwhelmed by the tragedy and fear that their suffering will never end. It seems to me vital that somehow we retain a sense of hope for the future. A fact that we must not lose sight of is that, however dreadful the catastrophe, the majority of people do recover; indeed, some are even strengthened by their ordeal.'[4]

The educational function and potential of the post disaster Newsletter, whether based on academic learning or personal experience, is a very valuable but probably under-stated one.

Forum to share

The most important function and the primary purpose of the Newsletter is to provide a forum in which the victims of a disaster can share their feelings, sorrows and hopes with each other. It can be a great source of strength and comfort for people to realise that they are not alone in their grief. For those who chose to contribute letters, poems or articles, the actual process of committing things to paper can, in itself, be therapeutic.

A selection of parts of some of the letters sent to, and published in *Piper-Line* attest to this fact.

From Piper-Line 2:

'This letter is to let you know that I feel it is good to start a Newsletter. It lets everyone know what is happening and it makes me feel that I am not alone ... I just keep thinking that it wasn't fair that he should die so young and leave us ... I feel so angry that he will never see [his children] grow up ... I know I must keep going for I am all they have got left ... I'll make sure he would be proud of his children, they give me the will to carry on. They are part of him and I'll always have that.'

From Piper-Line 4:

'My husband was killed on Piper Alpha. We would have been married for twenty years in August. I don't know if what I have written will make much sense, I just felt the words come out.

God bless all of you at *Piper-Line* and thank you for the Newsletters. When I read them, I know I am not alone.

That Sunday, his last, he didn't want to go, that day he wasn't happy about going. I told him to stay, to see the doctor for a few weeks off, but he wasn't ill, he just wanted to stay with us, he would be letting someone down if he didn't go and he couldn't do that. So he went laughing, not a real care in the world ... Was it "meant to be" his never coming home, we'll never know. Someone told me it was God's will. This I don't and never will believe. We have him home now, laid at last peacefully to rest. It was November 5th, the day after our daughter's tenth birthday. He always told her he'd be home for her birthday, he didn't let her down ... God be with us all, give us strength and courage to see these painful times through.'

And in the same issue one of the survivors wrote:

'I felt it was time I put pen to paper to thank you all for your hard work producing the Newsletter. I look forward to it coming to me.

Since July 6th things have not been easy for anyone as we all know. Maybe it hasn't made us better people, but one very important aspect which has changed in me is the unique understanding of anyone else who has been involved in a disaster of any type. Like most people I was shocked with the news of the Bradford fire and the *Herald of Free Enterprise* capsize, but since the Piper I have a new understanding of the feelings of victims and families ... Now with the recent disaster I feel I can relate only too well to the victims' situation ...'

People also used the letters page to share their deepest concerns, as in this extract from a widow writing to *Piper-Line 6*.

'I felt things were taken out of my hands - I knew I could not see the body; I was given no choice as to where the death was to be registered; everything seemed to have to be done so quickly. I know getting his body back was an added bonus and I should be grateful for this, but because I could not see him, at times I still wonder if it was him in that coffin. I do know this is daft, and that the police were very particular in identifying bodies through medical and dental records; but I still have no proof because I could not see him. It's a vicious circle really; I couldn't see him; I didn't want to see the body, but I'm still not truly convinced ...'

Also in *Piper-Line 6* two people chose to highlight the benefits of sharing. The first extract is from a sister whose brother died and the second from a wife who lost her husband:

'... But all this hardship has made me stronger than before, it's made me realise I love my other brothers and sister more now than ever. I don't take life for granted anymore because it goes on just the same, the only sad thing is that people forget so easily. All I can add to my letter is you who have been bereaved are not alone ...'

The second extract comes at the end of a long and detailed letter.

'... I hope you don't mind my going on and on in this letter but it is the first time in eight months I have written down my thoughts. Although relatives and friends are a great comfort and help, no one knows how you really feel inside.

Thank you for writing the *Piper-Line*, like Mrs F said in her letter in *Piper-Line 4* at least you know you are not alone in your thoughts or how you feel.'

Children's page

The social workers of the Piper Outreach Team decided to try to use the Newsletter as a means of reaching the children whose fathers had been killed in the disaster.

Taking advice from an educational psychologist, they developed the idea of a special children's page and invented the character of Bosey Badger. An artist provided some sketches of a friendly looking badger and these were reproduced as logos at the top of the page. The character was drawn to appeal to young children all over the UK but had perhaps an extra significance in the North East of Scotland where the word 'bosey' is a colloquialism meaning 'cuddle'.

The children were encouraged to fill the blank page with a poem, a drawing or a story and send it back to Bosey Badger. This was then printed in the next issue and the children were also sent a pencil and badger badge with a personal letter from 'Bosey'.

This attempt to encourage younger children to write or draw thoughts and feelings they might otherwise internalise and to share them with others proved remarkably successful.

The resulting pictures and poems were among the most poignant and moving of all the contributions received by the Piper Outreach team.

One twelve year old sent a drawing of an oil rig and the following verse:

'How well I remember the sixth of July
Including my father, many men did die
All of which were loved by you and by me,
And all of them were killed in that tragic sea.

I last saw my father on the 29th June
His last words to me were I'll see you all soon.
I love my father wherever he may be
And while up in Heaven I'm sure he loves me.'

Another sent a sketch representing the local Aberdeen Football Club players on their pitch and the accompanying text:

'I miss my dad he used to take me to the football match my dad is an angel now he dos not pay to go now he looks at the football from heven my brother and me gave him football flowers when he got buryed.'

The idea of the children's page has been taken up by those involved after the Hillsborough disaster in their newsletter, *Interlink*.

Overall the Newsletter is one of the most favourably commented on pieces of work following a disaster. If it can inform, educate and provide a space for sharing then it can be a valuable asset for people affected by a disaster in their attempts to come to terms with its effect on their lives.

Points for discussion

1. Discuss the various functions a newsletter can perform.

2. What problems might arise around the issue of editorial control? How might these be resolved?

3. Consider the balance between the beneficial aspects of sharing through a newsletter against the possibility that some of the contents may cause distress to the recipients.

4. Are there other developments, like the children's page, which might be worth incorporating in future similar publications?

References

1. Stewart, Michael, (1988) Survivors who must turn tragedy into opportunity. *Social Work Today*, 11th August.
2. Renzenbrink, Irene, (1988) After the Shootings: Disaster Recovery in Melbourne, Australia. Paper presented at 'International Conference on Grief and Bereavement', July.
3. *Piper-Line 2*, November 1988. Grampian Region (Social Work Department).
4. *Piper-Line 6*, July 1989. Grampian Region (Social Work Department).

Chapter 13

Offering a wider service

Introduction

One of the criticisms most often voiced about the social work input following a disaster does not concern its relevance or effectiveness but more often its absence in relation to those bereaved tragically, in less spectacular circumstances, prior to the disaster. This criticism is certainly valid, if a little unfair. Prior to the Bradford Football Ground disaster, social work had not conceived of a such a central role for itself in a post-disaster scenario. Emergency guidelines, where they had a role for social work at all, saw them as helping with rehousing or delivering emergency fuel supplies following a flood or similar natural occurence. Social work agencies have largely developed this post disaster role of their own volition, and each disaster brings new lessons, and additional areas of offering help and assistance are uncovered.

It nonetheless remains true that the differences between an individual bereavement in tragic circumstances and one in the context of a disaster are principally differences of scale and media attention. For the individuals concerned, the effects are very similar. If someone is killed suddenly and tragically in an accident at work or in a car crash, the traumatic effects on those bereaved are just as severe as on those bereaved by a disaster.

Post disaster

While the criticism that no such service was available in an area prior to a disaster has some justification, an even more powerful argument can be advanced that subsequently, at least, a similar service and effort should be available to those bereaved in tragic circumstances, but on an individual basis.

Once it has been established that those bereaved in sudden and unexpected circumstances can benefit from post disaster help and counselling, and also that the basic skills and expertise of social workers are appropriate and adaptable to that task, then it becomes morally difficult to justify not offering such a service in the future to the wider population.

The principal reason most often advanced for not continuing a service is one of finance. It is undoubtedly true that staffing and adequately resourcing a permanent bereavement, or critical incident team, would be a very expensive additional burden in a time when local authority funds are under restraint.

Balanced against the financial consideration, however, must be the fact that in many parts of the country social service staff have now had experience after a disaster of helping the bereaved and survivors. Other authorities, realising that disasters strike indiscriminately, have arranged training for their social workers so that teams are ready to become operative should the need arise.

Having trained and experienced staff able to offer skilled help to people in the wake of a traumatic incident, and then not utilising this, scarcely seems the best way of deploying resources.

So recognising the need for, and the value of such a service, is combined increasingly with the ability to deliver the service to those in need of it, and is restrained principally by financial considerations.

Given this scenario, it may be that the local authorities need to address the question of how such a service can be most effectively organised, rather than of whether there should be a service at all. The best method of organising this kind of service may well be one that does not commit the authority to the entire funding of it.

Establishing a service

Having decided in principle to establish a bereavement service, or the wider based traumatic incident service, a number of organisational options are available.

First, a social work department could establish a specialist team, or number of teams, to deal exclusively with those who would come into that category. In financial terms this would be the most costly of options, and the nature of the work would almost certainly mitigate against the staff remaining in post for extended periods. Perhaps most significantly, however, it would exclude many experienced and willing people not in the direct employ of the local authority.

A second option would be for the local authority to hand the entire task over to the voluntary sector. There is an enormous amount of expertise and experience in this sector, perhaps most obviously with organisations such as Cruse, the Compassionate Friends, Associations of Mental Health and the Samaritans. Local authorities often already grant assist such organisations and this could be increased where and when necessary. The difficulty with this approach might lie in achieving a consistency of service throughout a large geographical area. Because of their very voluntary nature their spread of members may be patchy in parts. Additionally, guaranteeing a constancy of service may be more difficult for voluntary organisations than it would be for a local authority.

A third option would be to release social work staff from their teams for some additional training and for them subsequently to take a number of bereaved or traumatised clients on as part of their regular case load. This option would have the advantage that should a disaster occur, then trained and experienced social workers should be readily available. The problem with this model may lie in the area of priority allocation, but this is a problem not unknown already in social work.

A fourth option would be to seek a combination of the voluntary and statutory sectors. A whole variety of models could be constructed around this joint approach. Perhaps the most obvious one would be for local authority staff to provide the co-ordinating role, linking up with the voluntary agency staff who would actually carry out most of the work. A slight refinement of this could provide for a small 'core' team of full-time staff working with a much larger 'cluster' team drawn principally from the voluntary sector, on an as required and as available basis.

The advantages of this type of approach would be to have the consistency and ready availability of a full-time team combined with the experience, skill and local base of the voluntary sector staff. It would require a financial commitment from the local authority, but perhaps a more manageable commitment than some other options. It would allow a specialist service to be available for those bereaved or otherwise involved in traumatic incidents who wished to avail themselves of it, and the service would be available when required and not subject to competing claims from other areas of work.

Some developments have taken place when disaster teams have ended their work. In Dover, where help following the *Herald of Free Enterprise* disaster was centred, a Counselling Centre came into being. This was principally an amalgam of Cruse, Relate (Marriage Guidance) and the Kent Council on Addiction, and the counsellors were drawn from these organisations. The management of the Centre was through an unpaid Board of Directors drawn from the voluntary sector, local authorities, local business and the churches. Some financial help was forthcoming from the local authorities but self financing through fund raising was a central task of the Directors.

Following the Piper Alpha disaster, the local Regional Council undertook to examine the prospect of a bereavement counselling service in the Grampian area. The team manager of the Piper Outreach Team was given the task of investigating the various options and the possible demands which would be placed upon such a service.

Conclusion

From Bradford to Dover, from Kings Cross to Piper Alpha, from Lockerbie to Hillsborough, social workers have played an important role in the care and support of those bereaved and those who survived.

The experience of those social workers and the testimony of those with whom they worked, both suggest that their skills and experience are of value to, and valued by, those with whom they seek to work.

It is unlikely that in the event of future disasters social service departments will not offer assistance in the aftermath, and the growing trend of departments to pre-train staff with this in mind seems to confirm this. It may be that when emergency plans are re-drawn in the future, the role of social work in the aftermath of a disaster will be formally included and acknowledged.

Whether such a service is extended to offer help to those bereaved or traumatised in less dramatic circumstances is a matter of political will and financial commitment, but it is an option that requires serious consideration and for which demand is likely to grow. Finally, those who are bereaved by, or who survive a disaster are subject to the most terrible of experiences and traumas. They can be supported in these and helped through them by skilled and thoughtful intervention.

The task is neither simple nor easy, but it is also not without reward and satisfaction for those who offer the help. There are many people who can help in such circumstances but not least among these are social workers whose skills, training and experience have been shown to be of assistance to the bereaved, the grieving, and the traumatised in the wake of a disaster.

Points for discussion

1. Can you envisage preparatory work and training for an emergency combined with the development of a counselling service for the bereaved and the survivors of non-public accidents (eg fires, road accidents)? How would such a service operate?

2. What are the similarities and the differences between social work in the wake of large-scale disasters and social work following less-publicised accidents?

Social Network Analysis

The case material in this series is based on social network analysis. During the past decade social workers and others in the helping professions have stressed the importance of understanding social networks. For example, it is important to recognise the importance of informal care as well as formal services.

Social network analysis is a new method of systematically measuring social networks. Part of this method consists in asking clients to keep diaries for a monitored period, usually a fortnight. Some months later the exercise is repeated. The diaries are focused on finding out the people, places and activities that are important to clients in daily living. Services are then evaluated in this context. Other 'information components', as they are called, include details of the client's social setting, the client's views and the views of the client's main support person at home (e.g. parent in the case of a child, son or daughter, perhaps, in the case of an elderly person) and assessments of the client's features of performance in interests.

Social network analysis is useful in research, for management and for monitoring services, as well as for individual practitioners. Its research applications are expressed in *Applied Social Network Analysis* (Costello, 1987). Its use for practitioners is described in *Introducing Network Analysis in Social Work* (Jessica Kingsley, 1990). Dr Philip Seed is the author of both books.

Key to network diagrams

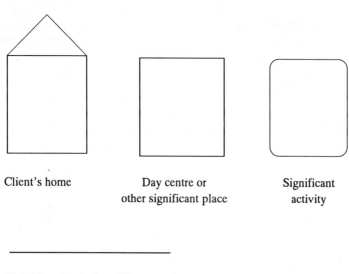

Client's home

Day centre or
other significant place

Significant
activity

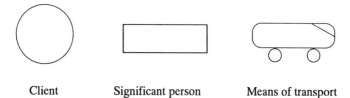

Visit (direction indicated by arrows)

Client

Significant person

Means of transport

Introducing Network Analysis in Social Work

Philip Seed

ISBN 1 85302 034 6 155 pages hardback
ISBN 1 85302 106 7 paper

This new textbook is designed for social workers and others in social work practice as a guide to the application of a systematic method for understanding and using social networks. As the importance of informal as well as formal care is more widely recognised, social workers and others in the helping professions have come to see the services they provide more and more in the context of the people, places and activities that are significant to the client's daily life.

In part one, social network analysis is studied generally; part two deals with specific applications of network analysis. Finally, the role of day care is studied, and procedures suggested for routine reviews using social network analysis.

CONTENTS 1. Introduction. **Part 1. General.** 2. What are social networks? 3. What do we mean by analysis? 4. Techniques. **Part 2. Specific applications.** 5. Fieldwork assessments. 6. Assessments prior to discharge from a residential establishment and follow-up review. 7. People leaving long-stay hospitals. 8. Day care. 9. Regular reviews. 10. Conclusion - the future. 11. Appendices. Index.

Philip Seed has taught social workers in the use of applied social network analysis under the auspices of the Central Council for Education and Training in Social Work, and this book was based on this work. He is Senior Research Fellow and Honorary Lecturer at the University of Dundee. He was previously at the University of Aberdeen. He has published many social work books and is currently Editor of the *Case Studies for Practice* series. This book should be read in conjunction with contributions to that series.

Case Studies for Practice

Series Editor: Philip Seed

This series draws together case material from social research to illuminate and explore vital issues in social work practice. Each volume in the series focuses on valuable material which has been collected in the course of research, especially research into social networks. The series is intended to be particularly useful for students on CQSW and CSS courses as well as for in-service training. At the same time, it discusses issues of concern to policy makers and practitioners.

Day Services for People with Mental Handicaps
2nd edition
Compiled by Philip Seed
ISBN 1 85302 039 7 103 pages 210 x 145 paper
Case Studies for Practice 1
Taking a social network approach, the cases presented show the extent to which the limits of community care can be and are stretched to provide the services needed by the mentally handicapped and those who care for them. Cases are grouped to illustrate particular topics. The first chapter examines day care in the lives of two people with mental handicaps five years after leaving long-stay hospitals. Chapters two and three deal with much neglected topics: the situation of the elderly mentally handicapped, and that of their even older carers. The functioning of the day care setting is then explored, and the ambiguous role and potential exploitation of a particular group - the very mild mentally handicapped - within it. A new final chapter for this second edition broadens the field of study by examining day services in rural areas.

The book will be of interest to students of social work and to social workers themselves, particularly those in in-service training for residential and day care staff, and on CSS and CQSW courses, and all those concerned with the better management of day care services.

'It is good to be able to recommend this small and well presented volume at a time when there is a positive ferment of ideas and much sustained effort going into improving resources and creating effective networks. Illuminating and fundamental points emerge as one proceeds; the issues raised for discussion at the end of each section are of great value.'

- Link-Up

Day Services for People with Severe Handicaps
Compiled by Philip Seed
ISBN 1 85302 013 3 128 pages paper
Case Studies for Practice 2
The second book in the series focuses on people with severe handicaps. The word 'severe' is used to include those who might be described in technical terms as having 'profound' or 'multiple' handicaps. In practical terms it is taken to mean people unable to perform most self-management or basic daily living tasks without substantial assistance. The book starts by contrasting the lifestyles of two teenagers with multiple handicaps. Both have cerebral palsy and are confined to wheelchairs, but in terms of background are quite different. The next section looks at broader issues, including the quality of communication between parents and the centre; the relevance of visits from the centre to other places; part-time attendance; the social function of centres; and whether educational activities at a centre can compensate for a lack of educational opportunity during schooling. After this the problem of respite for carers is studied. The closing chapters look at the different situations of individual clients: one who lives in a hostel but maintains parental contact; one who is physically fit but has a severe learning difficulty and one approaching 60 but with a degenerative condition leading to multiple disabilities.

Towards Independent Living: Issues for Different Client Groups
Compiled by Philip Seed
ISBN 1 85302 018 4 128 pages paper
Case Studies for Practice 3
There is an important social dimension to preparation for independent living. It is not just about learning how to open a tin of beans. In essence it is about social relationships and developing a better quality of life through social relationships. Clients should be enabled to be appropriately dependent on others and to allow others to be appropriately dependent on them. This book explores the ways in which this can be brought about.

The first chapter considers the outcomes for a group of young people who had a history of residential child care, followed by experience in a hostel specifically intended to enable them to live 'more independently' in the community. The next chapters consider adults with special needs: first, epileptic adults during and after intensive training in a hostel, and second, a group of people who had attended an adult training centre on a part-time basis. Next there is a study of the benefits that adults who have been mentally ill can gain in learning to cope independently in society from attending a voluntary-run club at a day centre. Finally, 'independent living' is looked at in connection with the care of elderly people.

Jessica Kingsley Publishers, 118 Pentonville Road, London N1 9JN

HIV and AIDS: A Social Network Approach
Compiled by Roger Gaitley and edited by Philip Seed
ISBN 1 85302 025 7 128 pages paper
Case Studies for Practice 4

This book examines the question of how professionals can best care for people whose HIV antibody positive status touches on so many of society's fears and taboos. Taking a social network approach, it draws on recent case material to explore the lives of people affected - directly or indirectly - by HIV and AIDS. The material comes from work in diverse areas: an agency making contact with 'rent' boys; direct work with drug users, some of whom are - or have partners who are - HIV positive; infants with HIV and their carers (including foster and adoptive parents) and the issues of confidentiality which arise; a group for relatives of people with HIV; and work exploring how potential social workers and other carers have to promote positive attitudes towards HIV and AIDS, as well as risk-free lifestyles.

By taking account of the people, activities and environments in his or her life, a total picture emerges of where a person finds key supports. The picture includes social, legal, health and interpersonal networks, describes where they complement, overlap and conflict, and illuminates the effects of the progression (if any) of the HIV infection in the person's life. The task of caring for the person, without further marginalising them in society, demands that these networks are understood and exploited to their full potential.

Respite: A Social Network Approach
Philip Seed
ISBN 1 85302 061 3 paper
Case Studies for Practice 7

of related interest

How to Get Equipment for Disability
Compiled by Michael Mandelstam

ISBN 1 85302 095 8   504 pages paperback

This important new book is set to become an essential reference source for anyone prescribing, advising or choosing from the vast range of equipment now available. Written under the auspices of the Disabled Living Foundation and the Nuffield Provincial Hospitals Trust, *How to Get Equipment for Disability* provides detailed information on

* what type of equipment is available
* who prescribes it
* what professionals are involved
* the referral procedure
* supply and delivery
* maintenance and follow-up.

The book will prove invaluable to GPs, district nurses, occupational therapists, physiotherapists, speech therapists, community nurses, health visitors, continence advisers, social workers, rehabilitation and mobility officers, consultants, ward sisters, environmental health officers, housing improvement officers, special education needs advisers and teachers, employment service DAS teams, residential and nursing home owners, and disabled people and their carers. All sections deal with regulations, legislation, circulars, White Papers and government reports in England and Wales, Scotland and Northern Ireland. The guide also includes a comprehensive directory of manufacturers and suppliers.

CONTENTS. PART I - 1. Daily living. 2. Housing adaptations. 3. Home nursing equipment. 4. Mobility equipment (a) wheelchairs (b) walking aids (c) vehicle scheme. 5. Footwear. 6. Orthotic equipment. 7. Prosthetic appliances. 8. Incontinence appliances. 9. Dental appliances. 10. Optical appliances. 11. Oxygen/respiratory equipment. 12. Renal dialysis equipment. 13. Diabetic equipment. 14. Hearing aids. 15. Stoma appliances. 16. Communication aids. 17. Residential home provision. 18. Private nursing home provision. 19. Medical equipment (in general) provision. 20. Educational provision of equipment. 21. Employment provision. PART II - Directory of manufacturers and suppliers

Published by Jessica Kingsley Publishers and Kogan Page for the Disabled Living Foundation

Research Highlights in Social Work

This topical series of books examines areas currently of particular interest to those in social and community work and related fields. Each book draws together a collection of articles on different aspects of the subject under discussion - highlighting relevant research and drawing out implications for policy and practice.

The project is under the general· direction of Professor Gerard Rochford.

Social Work: Disabled People and Disabling Environments
Edited by Michael Oliver
ISBN 1 85302 042 7 160 pages hardback
Research Highlights in Social Work 21
This new volume explores the social work response to the various aspects of work involving people with disabilities.

CONTENTS: Foreword, Tom Clarke. Editorial, Michael Oliver. 1. The social context of disability, Vic Finkelstein. 2. The changing context of social work practice, Bob Sapey. 3. The OPCS reports, Paul Abberley. 4. Disability and new technology, Paul Cornes. 5. Social work practice in traditional settings, Patrick Phelan. 6. Social work in an organisation of disabled people, Etienne d'Aboville. 7. Housing and independent living, Bernie Fiedler. 8. Social work with disabled children and their families, Caroline Glendenning. 9. Disabled young people, Michael Hirst. 10. Disability in adulthood, Ann Shearer. 11. Ageing with a disability, Gerry Zarb. 12. A view from the States, Irving Zola/Harlem Hahn.

Social Work and the European Community
The Social Policy and Practice Contexts
Edited by Malcolm Hill
ISBN 1 85302 091 5 226 pages hardback
Research Highlights in Social Work 23
The approaching creation of the single European Market in 1992 has heightened awareness of the growing integration of the European Community, which has major implications for social problems and social services. There is likely to be increased movement of social service users, social workers and of practice ideas. This book outlines the institutions of the European Community and their impact on social policy and social work. An analysis is made of the similarities and differences in approaches to public welfare, social service organisation and social work education within the social and political contexts of the member states of the EC. Finally, attention is given to a number of social work issues to examine how these are tackled within the EC. Such topics include community development, juvenile justice, child abuse, family policy and services for elderly people.

Poverty, Deprivation and Social Work
Edited by Ralph Davidson and Angus Erskine
ISBN 1 85302 043 5 hardback
Research Highlights in Social Work 22

New Information Technology in Management and Practice
Edited by Gordon Horobin and Stuart Montgomery
ISBN 1 85091 022 7 148 pages hardback
RHSW 13

Why Day Care?
Edited by Gordon Horobin
ISBN 1 85302 049 4 112 pages paper
ISBN 1 85302 000 1 hardback
RHSW 14

Performance Review in Social Work Agencies
Edited by Joyce Lishman
ISBN 1 85302 017 6 hardback
RHSW 20

Child Care: Monitoring Practice
Edited by Isobel Freeman and Stuart Montgomery
ISBN 1 85302 005 2 136 pages hardback
RHSW 17

Privatisation
Edited by Richard Parry
ISBN 1 85302 015 X hardback
RHSW 18

Social Work and Health Care
Edited by Rex Taylor and Jill Ford
ISBN 1 85302 016 8 144 pages hardback
RHSW 19

Evaluation: 2nd Edition
Edited by Joyce Lishman
ISBN 1 85302 006 0 144 pages hardback
RHSW 8

Living with Mental Handicap: Transitions in the Lives of People with Mental Handicap
Edited by Gordon Horobin and David May
ISBN 1 85302 004 4 176 pages hardback
RHSW 16

Developing Services for the Elderly: Second Edition
Edited by Joyce Lishman and Gordon Horobin
ISBN 1 85091 002 2 hardback
ISBN 1 85091 003 0 paper
RHSW 3

Sex, Gender and Care Work
Edited by Gordon Horobin
ISBN 1 85302 001 X 176 pages hardback
RHSW 15

The Family: Context or Client?
Edited by Gordon Horobin
ISBN 1 85091 026 X 160 pages paper
RHSW 12

Responding to Mental Illness
Edited by Gordon Horobin
ISBN 1 85091 005 7 114 pages paper
RHSW 11

Approaches to Addiction
Edited by Joyce Lishman and Gordon Horobin
ISBN 1 85091 000 6 hardback
ISBN 1 85091 001 4 paper
RHSW 10

Jessica Kingsley Publishers, 118 Pentonville Road, London N1 9JN

Social Work in Rural and Urban Areas
Edited by Joyce Lishman
ISBN 0 9505999 8 0 152 pages paper
RHSW 9

Social Work with Adult Offenders
Edited by Joyce Lishman
ISBN 0 9505999 4 8 184 pages paper
RHSW 5

Collaboration and Conflict: Working with Others
Edited by Joyce Lishman
ISBN 0 9505999 6 4 198 pages paper
RHSW 7

Social Work Departments as Organisations
Edited by Joyce Lishman
ISBN 1 85302 008 7 112 pages paper
RHSW 4

Working with Children
Edited by Joyce Lishman
ISBN 1 85302 007 9 164 pages paper
RHSW 6

Handbook of Theory for Accredited Practice Teachers in Social Work
Edited by Joyce Lishman
ISBN 1 85302 098 2   200 pages paper

As part of the general move towards accreditation and greater professionalism, Practice Teachers (supervisors) will from now on have to be accredited and undergo some training and practice teaching. This handbook has been commissioned to provide the theoretical base that Practice Teachers will need.

CONTENTS Part I - Models of understanding human development. 1 Attachment theory, Jane Aldgate, Oxford University. 2. Life stages theory, Alastair Gibson, RGIT. 3. Psychodynamic approach, Judith Brearley, Edinburgh University. 4. Structural/conflict models, Ann Davis, Birmingham University. 5. Loss and bereavement, Gerard Rochford, Aberdeen University. 6. Contributions from other disciplines to social work, Pauline Hardiker, Leicester University. Part II - Models of social work intervention. 7. Behavioural, Barbara Hudson, Oxford University. 8. Crisis theory, Kieran O'Hagan, Leeds Social Services. 9. Task centred, Peter Marsh, Sheffield University. 10. Counselling. a) Cognitive, Windy Dryden, Goldsmith's College. b) Psychodynamic, Michael Jacobs, Leicester University. 11. Community social work, Stuart Watts, Grampian Social Work Department. 12. Life space work, Colin Keenan, RGIT.

Joyce Lishman teaches in the School of Social Studies, Robert Gordon's Institute of Technology. She was previously in the Department of Social Work at Aberdeen University, where she edited the Research Highlights in Social Work series.

Gazing into the Oracle
The Delphi Method and its Application to Social Policy and Public Health
Edited by Michael Adler and Erio Ziglio
ISBN 1 85302 104 0 220 pages hardback
The Delphi method (or Delphi technique) is essentially an exercise in group communication which allows a number of individuals to deal with a complex problem or task simultaneously.

This introductory book will make the reader acquainted with the special uses of the Delphi method in social planning. It discusses important methodological and practical issues which need to be applied if the technique is to be applied successfully (for example the important aspect of computerisation); it illustrates the use of the technique by presenting case studies, and assesses the potential of the method for social policy and planning.

CONTENTS: PART 1 - THEORY AND METHODS. 1. An Outline of the Delphi Method and its relationship to other forms of decision-making and forecasting, Erio Ziglio. 2. Theoretical, methodological and practical issues arising out of the Delphi Method, David Gustafson and Armando Rotundi. 3. Computer Based Delphi Process, Murray Turoff and Starr R Hiltz. PART 2 - APPLICATIONS. 4. The use of the Delphi Method in constructing scenarios for the future of mental health care in the Netherlands, Rob Bijl. 5. Delphi Method in planning the services for the elderly, Giovanni Bertin. 6. Computerisation of the social security system, Michael Adler and Roy Sainsbury. 7. The use of qualitative techniques in maternity services: an Andalusian case study, Manuel Arantas. 8. The use of the Delphi Method in the forecasting of accidents in the year 2000, E F van Beeck. 9. Delphi Estimates on clients' perceptions of family planning services, Mauro Niero. 10. Learning from case studies: the way ahead, Michael Adler and Erio Ziglio.

Violence Against Social Workers
Dan Norris with Carol Kedward
With a foreword by Harriet Harman, MP
ISBN 1 85302 041 9 176 pages
In this new book, Dan Norris discusses the explanations for, the incidence of and the nature of violence against social workers. He surveys and comments on the existing literature on violence and discusses the research which has been done into its circumstances and causes. The attitudes of social workers themselves - the reluctance to report even serious incidents, the phenomenon of 'self-blame', and the response of their managers - are examined in the results of a specially conducted survey. Social workers' place in society and the way in which they function is central to the issue; this book looks at the effect of how they work, their attitudes to clients and the problems cause by poor management and insufficient resources and information. Finally, the author explores in detail methods of controlling and reducing violence and the implications which such approaches may have for social work practice and administration at all levels in the future. The possible dangers arising from new strategies and technologies which appear to reduce the problem are identified, along with the legal responsibilities of social work management.

Counselling Adult Survivors of Child Sexual Abuse
Christiane Sanderson
ISBN 1 85302 045 1 192 pages hardback

Although little research has been specifically directed at retrospective treatment intervention with adult survivors, its importance is beginning to be recognised. *Counselling Survivors of Child Sexual Abuse* examines the theories which attempt to account for the occurrence of child sexual abuse, explains the traumatic impact of child sexual abuse, and looks at the ways in which these effects can be ameliorated and the adult healed. Treatment techniques and the role of the counsellor in employing these techniques are also discussed in such a way that the counsellor can make use of the book not only as a review of current theory, but also as a practical handbook for use with clients who may be adult survivors of child sexual abuse.

Christiane Sanderson lectures in psychology at the University of London. She is the founder of the Incest Survivor's Network, which puts clients in touch with survivor's groups all over the country and gives advice on setting these groups up. The ISN also deals with referrals passed on from the BBC, Childline and the social services. She is experienced in counselling adult survivors of child sexual abuse, both in groups and as individuals, and has run several workshops on the subject.